STUDENT LEARNING GUIDE

to accompany

BIOSPHERE 2000:
PROTECTING OUR GLOBAL ENVIRONMENT

"WHAT IS DIS ☆#@/G#?! A THREAT NOT TO RENEW OUR LEASE ON DIS PLANET?! DEY CAN'T DO THAT TO US.........CAN DEY?"

STUDENT LEARNING GUIDE

to accompany

BIOSPHERE 2000:
PROTECTING OUR GLOBAL ENVIRONMENT

Cheryl Puterbaugh
Donald Kaufman
Cecilia Franz
Miami University

HarperCollins*College*Publishers

The frontispiece is reprinted with special permission of King Features Syndicate.

STUDENT LEARNING GUIDE to accompany BIOSHPERE 2000: PROTECTING OUR GLOBAL ENVIRONMENT

by Cheryl Puterbaugh, Donald G. Kaufman and Cecilia Franz

 This book is printed on recycled paper as part of our ongoing efforts to address environmental concerns.

CONTENTS

PREFACE

Student Learning Guide -- The Origin

The Student Learning Guide began as all of the *Biosphere 2000* books did -- from suggestions generated by students in Dr. Kaufman's Environmental Science class. It was their suggestions which ultimately transformed this study guide into a learning tool. We believe that the chapter objectives, key concepts, chapter questions, and "putting principles into practice" sections will combine to make the information presented in the text more comprehensible. Accordingly, we are truly thankful to Dr. Kaufman's students for supplying us with what we believe to be a successful formula for this guide.

There are others to thank for their contributions to this book. Scott Bagley and Chris Carter's compilations of "Did You Know" facts and "Environmental Success Stories" have helped bring the information presented in the text to life. Scott, and Chris are all former students of Dr. Kaufman's, and their additions were key to the formation of this unique text.

A big thanks also goes to Lisa Taylor and Lisa Breidenstein, who have aided in the editing process. Their additions (and deletions!) to this text have been most valuable.

We believe that you will find that this guide to be a great learning tool. As with any tool, however, its worth is proven with use. So use this guide -- and remember, it was written with you, the student, in mind.

INTRODUCTION

A Learning Process

You've probably already been given lots of tips and techniques for studying. You've been told to schedule your time, get plenty of rest, eat the right foods, and read in a quiet environment. You know four different methods for taking notes in class and several more techniques for outlining chapters. You can study alone, or with a partner, or in a group.

But these things affect only the environmental and mechanical aspects of what's going on. They never get to the heart of the matter, which isn't how you study, but how you *learn*. All those study techniques can be useful, and certainly they're full of common sense, but they'll work only if you pair them with a real effort to learn. That's why this book isn't a study guide; it's a Learning Guide.

This Learning Guide is set up so that you can follow a step-by-step technique for learning. There isn't anything really original about this technique—it's just some tried-and-true practices plus some common sense ideas about how adults learn. There's a Chinese proverb:

> *I hear and I forget;*
> *I see and I remember;*
> *I do and I understand,*

It happens that what the Chinese and others have known intuitively for a long time has recently begun to be confirmed by science and statistics. For example, one study concluded that we remember

> 10% of what we read
> 20% of what we hear
> 30% of what we see
> 50% of what we see and hear
> 80% of what we say
> 90% of what we say as we act

According to these findings, if you do nothing more than attend class and read the assigned chapters you'll remember about half of the class content!

Five Steps to Learning: Making the Most of Your Senses

This Learning Guide is set up so that you can use all of your senses to help you learn. In conjunction with the readings in the textbook *Biosphere 2000* and your instructor's in-class lectures, the exercises and activities in this Learning Guide will help you follow a learning path that looks something like this:

1

- Understand the basic concepts.

- Add to those concepts the associated facts.

- Relate the concepts and facts to each other, and translate them into meaningful, useful knowledge.

This Learning Guide has taken those three basic tasks and turned them into five steps that are the foundation of a learning technique. Steps 1 & 2 correspond with the task of understanding the basic idea. Step 3 corresponds with the task of adding facts and figures to the idea. Steps 4 and 5 enable you to translate the information into personal and useful knowledge. We suggest that you follow this technique as you learn about the environment through reading *Biosphere 2000: Protecting Our Global Environment*.

Step 1: Read for Chapter Objectives

Study Principles:

1. Know what to expect from the chapter.
2. Think about the objectives as you read.

Before you read the chapter, you should already know the most important points that will be made. What do the authors want you to know? The Chapter Outline and the Learning Objectives will indicate the things that are important for you to know. For example, the first section in Chapter Three is "Why Do We Study Ecology?" It's a safe bet that in Chapter Three it'll be important to learn why we study ecology.

Step 2: Identify the Important Concepts

Study Principle:

Grasp the major concepts first.

Identifying the important concepts means making mental note of specific concepts as they appear and are elaborated on. The Key Concepts of each chapter can be identified in the chapter summary, or you can highlight them in the text as you read. These concepts will provide a framework for organizing all the facts (names, numbers, etc.) that you will need to learn in Step 3.

Step 3: Master the Facts

Study Principles:

1. Read the fact aloud or picture it in your mind.
2. Apply it to a major concept.
3. Say or write it in your own words.

The important facts you need to master in Step 3 are things like terms, numbers, names and places. Your knowledge of the facts are tested with Multiple Choice, True or False, Fill-in-the-Blank, and Short Answer questions. The Important Terms are also listed for each chapter.

You learn facts by figuring out some way to relate them to yourself or something you already know, by explaining them to someone else, by picturing them vividly in your mind, by reciting them, or by writing them in your own words. As you encounter each fact, you should associate it with a concept you identified in Step 2. Think about the fact—What does it really mean? What concept does it belong to and how does it fit in? Imagine what it looks like. For things that are alike, make sure you can tell what's different about them. For things that are parts of a whole, make sure you can tell how they fit together—and break down again. For things that are listed together, make sure you know how they relate to each other.

Examples are helpful at this point. It's easier to understand and remember an example drawn from a real-life situation than it is to memorize a dictionary definition. Examples also provide you with a mental framework, so by remembering the example, you remember the facts.

When you get to Step 4 you'll use these facts to support or illustrate your own discussion of these concepts.

Step 4: Analyze, Compare and Apply

Study Principles:

1. Practice relating the facts and concepts to each other.
2. Use examples to illustrate the concepts.
3. Back up your essays with the facts.

In this step you perform the higher-order learning tasks that are often tested with essay questions and research paper assignments. The Learning Guide uses Related Concepts and Thought Questions to provide you the opportunity to discuss your new knowledge.

Step 5: Put it into Practice

Study Principles:

1. Relate what you've learned to your own experience.
2. Explain what you've learned to someone else.

Without a personal experience which imparts significance to the concepts and facts that you learn, you can quickly forget the information. In fact, research has shown that you'll forget it in 48 hours. Step 5 is the final, important step, in which you use the information you have learned and make it part of your experience.

One of the best ways to put your learning into practice and make sure you've really got it, is to teach it to someone else. When you know you have to teach something, you learn it better, because you can't get by with a partial understanding. Try to arrange with a friend or classmate to teach them the material. If you can't do that, make use of the Suggested Activities sections in the Learning Guide. These activities are intended to give you a real-life framework for internalizing what you've learned.

To make all this work for you, you can follow these steps as you learn the material in *Biosphere 2000*. As you go through each of the exercises in this Learning Guide, you'll see one of the five icons that represent these steps at the beginning of each new section. The icon is there to remind you where you are in the learning process and what you should be doing.

We have also included interesting pieces of information in "Did You Know. . .?" boxes. These bits of not-so-trivial trivia help to bring some "real-world" perspectives to your academic study. You can also use them to amaze your friends with your environmental knowledge!

Here is one final piece of advice: feel free to write in this learning guide wherever you want. You will notice that we have left space for you to write in the outline and around the questions. Take advantage of this space to add information you think is important or to make any other notes that will be helpful to you. This learning guide was written to help *you* learn--don't hesitate to make it your own.

UNIT ONE

THE BIOSPHERE AND ENVIRONMENTAL SCIENCE

CHAPTER 1

Where Are We Now? An Overview of Environmental Problems

Chapter Outline

I. What is the Biosphere?

    A. Definition

        1. Thin Layer of Rock, Air, Water, and Soil Surrounding Earth

        2. Contains Conditions to Support Life

    B. Two Basic Components

        1. Biotic (Living), Characterized By:

                a. Cellular Structure

                b. Movement

                c. Growth

                d. Reproduction

                e. Response to Stimuli

                f. Evolve and Adapt

        2. Abiotic (Nonliving)

II. How Did the Biosphere Develop?

    A. Big Bang Theory

        1. Universe Arose from Hot Point Called Singularity

        2. Singularity Exploded and Space Began to Expand

3. As Expanding Universe Cooled, Particles and Matter Formed

4. As Gravity Caused Matter to Form Clumps, Galaxies Formed

B. Evolution Proceeded on Young Planet

1. Result of Organisms' Adaptations to Environmental Changes

2. Driving Forces

a. Mutations

b. Natural Selection

III. What Is the State of Biosphere I?

IV. What Are the Three Root Causes of Environmental Problems?

A. Population Growth

1. Exponential Growth

2. Over 5 Billion People on Earth

B. Abuse of Resource and Natural Systems

1. Renewable Resources

2. Nonrenewable Resources

C. Pollution

V. Why Do Uncontrolled Population Growth, Resource Abuse, and Pollution Occur?

    A. Worldview

        1. Person's/Society's Way of Perceiving Reality

        2. Comprised of Attitudes, Values, and Beliefs

        3. Reflected In and Transmitted Through Culture

    B. Dominant Western Worldview a Product of:

        1. Judeo-Christian Beliefs

        2. Use of Science

        3. Rise of Capitalism and Democracy

        4. Industrialization

VI.   What is the Environmental Revolution?

    A. Native American Lifestyle

    B. Aldo Leopold

        1. Author of *A Sand County Almanac*

        2. Idea of "Land Ethic" and "Stewardship"

VII. What Social and Environmental Factors Have Contributed to the Environmental Revolution?

VIII. How Has the Environmental Revolution Caused Us to Reassess Our Relationship with Nature?

    A. Development of Respect for the Worldview of Other Cultures

    B. Examination of the Words "Environment" and "Nature"

        1. Environment

            a. System of Interdependent Living and Non-living Systems

b. Includes All Physical, Biological, and Chemical Interactions

2. Nature

    a. Living Things Interacting with Earth's Nonliving Components

    b. Self-Sufficient System in which Life is Sustained in Dynamic Equilibrium

    c. Are Humans Part of Nature?

        1. If "No," then Anthropocentric View

        2. If "Yes," then Biocentric View

        3. If "Maybe," then Human Culture not Viewed as Natural

Learning Objectives

After learning the material in Chapter 1 you should be able to:

1. Describe the biosphere and explain how scientists believe it evolved.

2. Summarize the current state of the biosphere.

3. Identify the three root causes of environmental problems and explain how each relates to the current state of the biosphere.

4. Explain how environmental problems and the human activities that cause them are related to cultural attitudes, values, and beliefs.

5. Define what is meant by the environmental revolution and identify the social and environmental factors that have contributed to it.

6. Distinguish between a biocentric and an anthropocentric worldview.

7. Define "environment" and "nature" and distinguish between the two.

Did You Know . . . ?

On Earth Day, April 22, 1990, people celebrating in New York City left 160 tons of litter in Central Park.

Key Concepts

Read this summary of Chapter 1 and identify the important concepts discussed in the chapter.

The biosphere is the thin layer of air, water, soil, and rock that surrounds the earth and contains the conditions to support life. Scientists believe that the universe originated from an infinitely dense, infinitely hot point, called a singularity, in a big bang some 13 to 20 billion years ago. The Earth formed about 4.6 billion years ago from interstellar dust and gas. Life on earth is believed to have begun between 3.5 and 4 billion years ago, after the planet's surface cooled. Over the millennia the earth's living organisms evolved and diverged, adapting to changes in the nonliving environment. The process of evolution is driven by genetic mutations and natural selection. Mutations, random changes within the genetic material of an individual that can be passed off to that individual's offspring, are often harmful or result in changes that are not useful to the organism. Sometimes, however, a mutation causes an organism to differ in such a way that it is better suited to its environment than are other members of the population. Because it is more likely to survive and reproduce, passing on its genetic characteristics to its young, it is said to be "naturally selected for." Natural selection thus enhances an organism's chances for successful reproduction.

While change has been a constant characteristic of the planet throughout its history, humans have altered the planet in unprecedented ways. We have been able to modify our environment significantly through technology and social institutions, but we cannot control natural processes. As the current state of Biosphere I illustrates, *our earth environment sets limits on all creatures*. Natural catastrophes such as droughts and hurricanes, which may or may not be exacerbated by human actions, and worldwide problems such as global warming and stratospheric ozone depletion, indicate that we may have approached the earth's limits.

The three root causes of environmental problems are population growth, abuse of resources and natural systems, and pollution. Global population growth is exponential or geometric; increased growth in many parts of the world is stressing or exceeding the productive or supportive ability of local natural systems. In slow growth areas such as the United States, per capita consumption is so high that a single individual has a far greater impact on the environment than does an individual in a fast growth (generally poor) country. Resource abuse occurs when renewable resources are used in such a way that they cannot be regenerated; they are exploited to such an extent that they become depleted. Satisfying wants rather than needs can lead to resource abuse, as can technologies that harvest or exploit resources so completely or so efficiently that the resources cannot renew themselves. Pollution may be local, regional, or global in nature, and it may originate from natural or cultural sources. It is a mistake to suppose that pollution is a contemporary phenomena; humans (and other organisms) have always generated wastes. As long as populations were small, natural systems could degrade and recycle wastes. Contemporary societies, however, produce synthetic wastes and wastes in such large volumes that natural systems may be unable to recycle them.

Environmental problems arise from the interaction of natural and cultural systems. Accordingly, to solve environmental problems, individuals and societies must address the underlying cultural factors—attitudes, values, and beliefs—that cause the problems. Part of that process must be an examination of one's worldview, or way of looking at reality, which includes beliefs about the relationship of humans with the natural world.

The decade of the 1990s promises to be one of renewed commitment to environmental action. Humans must develop and encourage aspirations within the limits imposed by the environment. Ecological balance is the ultimate relationship humans must learn to maintain with nature. *No matter how far removed we become from direct contact with nature, we remain a part of it.* If our species is to survive and prosper, this contact must be nurtured.

Key Terms

abiota

anthropocentric view

big bang theory

biocentric view

biosphere

biota

environment

evolution

frontier mentality

land ethic

mutation

natural selection

nature

net primary productivity (NPP)

nonrenewable resource

pollutant

renewable resource

resource

sense of the earth

speciation

worldview

Environmental Success Story

After hearing of a manatee that had been injured by a motorboat, Lyle Solla-Yates, a ten-year-old from Miami Shores, Florida, started a group called "Pals of Wildlife" to raise money to help save animals. He was joined by 20 of his friends, who helped come up with ideas to raise money. They sold T-shirts that each club member helped design as well as pencils that had "Pals of Wildlife" printed on them. Other fundraisers included an "Earthday Birthday" party, where they planted trees, played games, and sold environmentally-oriented arts and crafts. As a result of their efforts, the group raised hundreds of dollars, which they donated to various environmental organizations.

True/False

1. The biosphere is composed of two distinct and entirely   T   F
   unrelated components, the abiota and the biota.

2. Living organisms evolve and adapt in response to changes in   T   F
   the environment because of an innate desire to survive.

3. Earth underwent significant change from the time of its   T   F
   formation until the appearance of life, approximately 3.5 to 4
   billion years ago, but the physical environment has remained
   relatively constant since then.

4. Resource consumption in affluent countries has a serious   T   F
   impact on the planet's natural systems.

5. Religion is not a significant factor in the development of a   T   F
   person's or society's worldview.

Fill in the Blank

1. About _____% of the world's resources are consumed by people living in developed nations.

2. A substance that adversely affects the quality of the earth's environment is a(n) _____ .

3. The belief that buildings and other things produced by humans are not natural is part of a(n) _____ view.

4. The worldview held by St. Francis of Assisi and other Christians saw humans as

   _____ .

5. Beginning at the end of the 18th century, _____ and _____ caused people to become separated from daily contact with the land, and they began to lose their sense of the earth.

Multiple Choice

Choose the best answer.

1. Which of the following terms describe opposite conceptions of humans' place in nature?
   A. biotic and abiotic
   B. biocentric and anthropocentric
   C. cultural and primitive
   D. consumerism and environmentalism

2. The biosphere
   A. is made up of the interacting regions of the atmosphere, hydrosphere, and lithosphere.
   B. includes any place where life can be found.
   C. is relatively small compared to the earth's total mass.
   D. All of the above are true.

3. The belief that humans are subject to all natural laws is characteristic of the _____ viewpoint.
   A. spaceship earth
   B. biotic
   C. anthropocentric
   D. biocentric

4. The three root causes of environmental problems are
   A. environmental degradation, decreasing species diversity, and population growth.
   B. consumerism, resource abuse, and increased consumption per capita.
   C. population growth, resource abuse, and pollution.
   D. industrialization, pollution, and population growth.

5. A key factor that contributed to the environmental revolution of the 1960s was
   A. writings, such as *Silent Spring* by Rachel Carson, that warned of environmental degradation.
   B. fear of global warming.
   C. a growing belief in anthropocentrism.
   D. All of the above are true.

Short Answer

1. What is the Spaceship Earth analogy?

2. Define the terms anthropocentric and biocentric in terms of a person's definition of what is natural.

3. What characteristics are shared, in general, by all living organisms?

4. What are renewable resources? What are nonrenewable resources?

5. What is net primary productivity (NPP)?

Thought Questions

Develop a complete answer for each of the following.

1. What is meant by the following statement? *Our earth environment sets limits on all creatures.* What viewpoint does this represent?

2. How do the abiota and biota interact with one another to influence the biosphere?

3. What is the prevailing scientific theory of how life on earth began? How did evolutionary processes produce the species on earth today?

4. How are the three root causes of environmental problems related?

5. What are the implications of the population growth race for people in developing countries? for non-human species? for nonrenewable resources?

6. What is the Western worldview and how has it affected the environment? What are the major factors that shaped the Western worldview?

14

7. What social and environmental conditions contributed to the environmental revolution of the 1960s and 1970s? How successful was the revolution?

Related Concepts

Describe the relationship. (There may be more than one.)

BETWEEN...	AND...
exponential growth	population
Biosphere I	Biosphere II
cultural systems	biosphere
ozone depletion	acid precipitation
Aldo Leopold	land ethic
frontier mentality	Native American beliefs

Did You Know . . . ?

1845: To avoid the waste and destruction of modern life, Henry David Thoreau withdraws to a cabin in the woods, later publishes *Walden*, a record of his thoughts and observations.

Suggested Activities

1. Exponential growth can be a tricky concept to grasp. To get a better understanding of how population numbers increase so dramatically, use your calculator to carry out the example given in Chapter One. If every day for a month you are given twice the amount you received the day before, starting with one penny, how much would you receive on the 30th day?

2. Research an environmental problem which has impacted you or someone you know. What factors led to its occurrence? What are the effects? What is being done to solve it?

3. What, to you, is the most serious environmental problem facing the world today? Think about why you feel this way - what beliefs and values do you hold that led you to conclude this? Write an essay or letter about your answer.

4. Take some time to think about your worldview and write a statement describing it. Think about the consequences of your beliefs, attitudes, and values. What sort of earth do you want to leave for your children and for all future generations to inherit? What will it take to make that legacy possible?

5. Start a microcosm and observe it for a few weeks or months. Fill a clean jar with water from a pond, lake, marsh or tidal pool, seal the jar so it is airtight, and place it on a windowsill where it will receive indirect sunlight. (Too much direct sunlight will make the jar too hot and kill the organisms inside.)

CHAPTER 2

And Where Do We Want to Go? Achieving a Sustainable Future

Chapter Outline

I. What Is a Sustainable and Sustaining Earth Society?

    A. Sustainable -- Human Behavior Acts to Maintain Health of Environment

    B. Sustaining -- Healthy Natural World Supports Rich Diversity of Life

    C. Standard of Living Equation

        1. $\text{Culture} \times \dfrac{\text{Resource Base}}{\text{Population}} = \text{Standard of Living}$

        2. Equation Reveals Reasons Behind Standard of Living Disparities

II. How Can We Act as Environmental Stewards?

    A. As Individuals

        1. Become More Knowledgeable about Area in Which We Live

        2. Contact with Nature

    B. Global Efforts

        1. Pool Knowledge

        2. Coordinate Actions

        3. Share What Planet Has to Offer

III. What Is Science?

    A. Scientific Inquiry -- Process of Knowing about the Natural World

Through:

    1. Observation

    2. Hypothesis

    3. Experiment

    4. Findings

    5. Significance

  B. Limitations of Scientific Inquiry

    1. Not Always Possible to Conduct a Controlled Experiment

    2. Tends to be Reductionist

    3. Limitation from Value-free Approach to Scientific Work

  C. Role of Scientists and Nonscientists

    1. Scientists Aid in Informed Decision-making

    2. Nonscientists Aid in Value Judgment

IV. What Is the Natural Science of Ecology?

  A. Definition

    1. Scientific Study of Structure, Function, and Behavior of Natural Systems

    2. Study Relationships of Organisms with Each Other and Environment

  B. Ecologists Attempt to Understand Ecosystems as Functioning Systems

V. What Is Environmental Science?

  A. Concerned with Interactions Between Natural/Cultural Systems

  B. Interdisciplinary

VI. What Methods Can We Use to Solve Environmental Problems?

A. Utilizes a 5-step Process

   1. Identify and Diagnose the Problem

   2. Set Goals and Objectives

   3. Design and Conduct a Study

   4. Propose Alternative Solutions

   5. Implement, Monitor, and Re-evaluate the Chosen Solution

B. Advantages to Use of Environmental Problem Solving

   1. Requires Communication among a Team to Solve Problems

   2. Preferred to the Longer and Costly Process of Litigation

C. Disadvantages to Use of Environmental Problem Solving

   1. Reactive Method of Problem Solving

   2. Damage Must Occur Before Problem Is Recognized

D. Environmental Problem Solving Differs From Scientific Inquiry

   1. Value Oriented

   2. Methodology

   3. Overall Goal

E. Environmental Activism

F. Litigation

VII. How Can We Minimize Environmental Problems?

    A. Stewardship Ethic

    B. Environmentally Sound Management

        1. Any Resource Can Be Managed in an Environmentally Sound Way

        2. Management Plan Minimizes or Prevents Environmental Degradation

        3. Development Sustainable when Resources are Conserved for Future Use

VIII. How Can We Implement Environmentally Sound Management?

    A. Pro-active Management of Resources

    B. Management Constructed Through Use of the Following Criteria:

        1. Stewardship Ethic

        2. Biocentric Worldview

        3. Understanding Natural System Dynamics

        4. Environmental Education

        5. Interdisciplinary Planning

        6. Data Based on Sound Natural and Social System Research

        7. Sociocultural Considerations

        8. Knowledge of Political Systems

        9. Sound Economic Analysis

        10. Maximum Public Participation

Learning Objectives

After learning the material in Chapter 2 you should be able to:

1. Appreciate and understand the need for both a sustaining and sustainable earth society.

2. Identify the standard of living/resource use equation, and define its components.

3. Determine the direct relationship of population growth and increased consumption per capita with resource abuse and increased environmental impacts (based on the resource use equation).

4. Determine positive steps individuals can take in order to become stewards of the earth.

5. Define science and the process of scientific inquiry.

6. Define environmental science, and describe the underlying value of its interdisciplinary nature.

7. Understand the cyclical nature of environmental problem solving, and describe each step in the process.

8. Differentiate between environmental problem solving and the scientific method.

9. Determine the advantages/disadvantages associated with the environmental problem solving method.

10. Recognize the need for implementing sound environmental management plans as a means of minimizing/avoiding environmental degradation.

Did You Know . . . ?

In China, people in urban areas are four to six times more likely to die of lung cancer than rural residents.

Key Concepts

Read this summary of Chapter 2 and identify the important concepts discussed in the chapter.

A sustaining and sustainable earth society is the goal to which we must dedicate ourselves if we are to preserve the planetary conditions we now enjoy. A stewardship ethic, in which humans act to care for and sustain natural systems and to conserve resources, is critical to achieving a sustainable society. Stewardship implies a knowledge of the land and of natural systems; one way to acquire that knowledge is to become familiar with a specific area -- its soils, climate, organisms, and so forth. You can do this simply by spending time observing an area and noting its characteristics, seasonal changes, vegetation, and the behavior of its resident animals.

One very important way of learning about the natural world is through science. The natural science of ecology views natural systems holistically, studying how all the individual parts interact with each other, and thus it can help us understand how culturally created stresses affect those systems. The scientific method is a value-free process that seeks answers to questions about the natural world. It relies on observation, the formation of hypotheses, and the design of experiments that can be repeated by other scientists. Although the scientific method is a very powerful tool, it cannot answer "why" questions (since these questions do not lend themselves to experimentation), nor can it be used to make value judgments ("Is what I observe good or bad?" "Given that a certain human action has a specific effect, should we continue or cease this action?"). "Why" questions and value judgments are the domain of the social sciences, humanities, and the arts.

Environmental science differs from the natural sciences because it takes into account human values and culture. Therefore, environmental science draws from both the natural sciences and the social sciences, the humanities, and the arts. Our challenge in solving environmental problems is to understand the underlying scientific principles and the consequences of interrupting natural processes through the long-term effects of our social actions. This focus on basic scientific concepts, coupled with an understanding of social processes, forms a basis on which to analyze, propose solutions to, and manage environmental problems.

Environmental problems can be solved through the careful, systematic use of problem-solving methods. Our five-step model can be followed by anyone interested in working for a better environment. The five steps of this model are: 1) identify and diagnose the problem; 2) set goals and objectives; 3) design and conduct a study; 4) propose alternative solutions; and 5) implement, monitor, and reevaluate the chosen solution. The quality of the environment depends on the decisions of its citizens and the choices we make in finding solutions to environmental problems. Problem-solving teams should be interdisciplinary, composed of people from many walks of life.

Environmental problems can be minimized or avoided through environmentally sound management which is based on the following ten criteria: 1) stewardship ethic; 2) biocentric worldview; 3) understanding of natural system dynamics; 4) environmental education; 5) interdisciplinary planning; 6) data based on sound natural and social system research; 7) sociocultural considerations; 8) knowledge of political systems; 9) sound economic analysis; and 10) maximum public participation. Environmentally sound management acknowledges that all forms of life on earth have value, opposes uncontrolled resource exploitation, promotes the wise use of resources, and minimizes waste and environmental damage. Because no one can predict what future generations will deem of value, the most important thing we can do is ensure a maximum of choice for future generations.

Key Terms

ecology

ecosystem

environmental science

environmentally sound management (ESM)

science

scientific inquiry

standard of living

sustainable earth society

sustaining earth society

Environmental Success Story

It seems as if there is at least one useful thing that comes from the chemicals that are dumped into our lakes and bays. Jeremy Lynch, a Toronto photographer, uses water from Lake Ontario to develop his pictures. He explains that the secret is hydroquinone, which is in diesel fuel and paint thinner, and is also the main component in the solution usually used to develop film. After sampling over 20 sites from different parts of the lake, he found one that worked--near a shipyard. The water from this spot develops an immersed negative in around 28 hours. Other waters with notable film-developing potential are New York City Harbor (26 hours) and Love Canal (3 hours).

True/False

1. The United States currently offers a good model of a sustainable and sustaining earth society.   T   F

2. Given sufficient funds for research and the development of advanced technologies, science will find effective solutions to environmental problems that are acceptable to all parties.   T   F

3. The most difficult, and the most easily overlooked, step of the problem solving model is the identification and diagnosis of the problem.   T   F

23

4. Litigation is the preferred method for solving environmental problems because it offers the best outcome for the environment (that is, it offers the best protection for the environment and natural systems).　　T　F

5. Environmental problem solving is relatively inexpensive and proactive while environmental management is costly and reactive.　　T　F

Fill in the Blank

1. For any society, its _____, _____, and _____ determine how that society uses resources and its resultant standard of living.

2. Observation, hypothesis development, and experimentation together comprise _____.

3. A(n)_____ is a self-sustaining community of organisms interacting with one another and with the physical environment within a given geographic area.

4. _____ is an adversarial process, in which opposing sides are represented by legal attorneys, that can be used to address environmental problems.

5. Environmentally sound management differs from environmental problems solving because it incorporates a(n) _____.

Multiple Choice

Choose the Best Answer

1. Based on the generalized model for average standard of living, which of the following societies will have the lowest standard of living?
   A. a society with a large population, a relatively small resource base, and cultural attitudes that encourage conservation, reuse, and recycling of resources.
   B. a society with a small population, a relatively large resource base, and cultural attitudes that encourage conservation, reuse, and recycling of resources.
   C. a society with a large population, a relatively small resource base, and cultural attitudes that encourage consumption of resources.
   D. a society with a small population, a relatively large resource base, and cultural attitudes that encourage consumption of resources.

2. A(n) _____ is designed to compare two situations that differ in a single variable.
   A. environmental problem solving model
   B. lawsuit
   C. controlled scientific experiment
   D. environmentally sound resource management model

3. The five steps of the problem solving model, in the correct order, are:
   A. set goals and objectives; identify and diagnose the problem; design and conduct a study; propose alternative solutions; implement, monitor, and evaluate the chosen solution.
   B. identify and diagnose the problem; set goals and objectives; design and conduct a study; propose alternative solutions; implement, monitor, and evaluate the chosen solution.
   C. design and conduct a study; identify and diagnose the problem; set goals and objectives; propose alternative solutions; implement, monitor, and evaluate the chosen solution.
   D. propose alternative solutions; set goals and objectives; identify and diagnose the problem; design and conduct a study; implement, monitor, and evaluate the chosen solution.

4. Which of the following is NOT a method for resolving difficult environmental issues and situations?
   A. environmental problem solving
   B. litigation
   C. environmentally sound management
   D. environmental activism

5. Environmental science differs from ecology in that it
   A. considers human values.
   B. defines a process for solving environmental problems.
   C. must sometimes take action on a problem or issue before all data are collected.
   D. all of the above.

Short Answer

1. What is a sustaining and sustainable earth society?

2. What are two ways that scientists ensure their research is free of bias or coercion?

3. What is an ecosystem?

4. Explain briefly how each of the following may play a role in environmental problem solving: ecology, theology, education, art, communication, history, political science, and economics.

5. What are the five steps of the environmental problem-solving model?

Thought Questions

Develop a complete answer for each of the following.

1. Explain the model for determining the average standard of living. What accounts for the wide disparity in standards of living around the world?

2. What does it mean to be a steward of nature?

3. What is scientific inquiry? What are its strengths and limitations?

4. What are the differences between the scientific method and environmental problem solving? What are the similarities? When is one more appropriate than the other?

5. Explain the three methods of solving environmental problems (five-step model, litigation, activism) and discuss why environmentally sound management is preferable to all three.

6. Describe the members of a typical environmental problem solving team. Explain why interdisciplinary planning is essential to the success of the environmental problem-solving method.

Related Concepts

Describe the relationship. (There may be more than one.)

BETWEEN...	AND...
hypothesis	principle
ethics	science
value judgments	environmental problems
litigation	environmental problem-solving model
environmental problem solving	environmentally sound management
scientific method	environmental problem solving

Did You Know . . . ?

Only two paper mills in the United States make newsprint from 100 percent recycled paper.

Suggested Activities

1. Write a letter to the editor (imaginary or not) of your local newspaper, encouraging citizens to adopt a stewardship ethic toward the environment.

2. Consider your own intended major or profession. How might you contribute to environmental problem solving and environmentally sound management?

3. Imagine you have been asked to solve an environmental problem. Develop the interdisciplinary team you would need to follow the environmental problem-solving model, and explain each of your choices.

4. Develop your own stewardship ethic by nurturing your sense of the earth. You might tend a garden, visit a national park or wilderness area, and search for wildflowers along roadsides or in vacant lots. Capture your thoughts and experiences through writing, art, or some other means of expression.

UNIT TWO

HOW THE BIOSPHERE WORKS

CHAPTER 3

Ecosystem Structure

Chapter Outline

I. Why Do We Study Ecology?

    A. Understand How Living Things Interact with Environment and Each Other

    B. Understand How Earth's Living Systems Maintain Integrity of the Biosphere

    C. Key to Environmental Problem Solving and Sound Management

II. What Are the Levels of Ecological Study?

    A. Individual

    B. Population

    C. Community

    E. Ecosystem

    F. Biome

    G. Biosphere

III. What Is an Ecosystem?

    A. Definition

        1. Self-sustaining, Self-regulating Community of Organisms

        2. Interacts with Physical Environment Within a Defined Geographic Space

B.   Undergoes Internal Change as a Result of Change to External Environment

IV. What Are the Components of an Ecosystem?

   A. Abiota, or Non-living Factors

      1. Energy

      2. Matter

      3. Physical Factors (Temperature, Humidity, Moisture, Light, Wind, Space)

   B. Biota, or Living Organisms

      1. Autotrophs

      2. Heterotrophs

V.   What Determines the Structure of Ecosystems?

   A. Abiotic Regulators

   B. Biotic Regulators

Learning Objectives

After learning the material in Chapter 3 you should be able to:

1. Appreciate the link between ecology and environmental problem solving.

2. Define ecosystem.

3. Identify biota and abiota as the basic components of ecosystem structure.

4. Understand how limiting factors determine the structure of ecosystems.

5. Understand how living organisms determine the structure of ecosystems.

6. Appreciate the regional, national, and international importance of the Lake Erie resource.

7. Identify the numerous environmental problems facing Lake Erie today.

8. Understand both the history of dealing with Lake Erie's environmental dilemmas, as well as future management plans designed to prevent the reappearance of such problems.

Did You Know . . . ?

Close to two million worms can be found in an area the size of a football field.

Key Concepts

Read this summary of Chapter 3 and identify the important concepts discussed in the chapter.

Solving environmental problems and developing environmentally sound management plans require an understanding of natural systems. Ecology can provide that understanding. Ecologists study the natural world at many levels: species, population, community, ecosystem, biome, and biosphere.

Ecosystems are life-perpetuating systems having structural components called the abiota and biota. The abiota consists of energy, matter, and physical factors such as light, heat, humidity, temperature, precipitation, shade, fire, salinity, and available space. Energy can neither be created nor destroyed but may be changed in form and may be moved from place to place, a principle known as the first law of energy or first law of thermodynamics. The second law of energy or second law of thermodynamics states that with each change in form, some energy is degraded to a less useful form and given off to the surroundings, usually as heat. Entropy refers to the tendency of natural systems toward dispersal or randomness.

Elements, substances that cannot be changed to simpler substances by chemical means, comprise all matter. Matter is neither created nor destroyed but its form may be changed and it can be moved from place to place, a principle known as the law of the conservation of matter.

The biota is composed of autotrophs (producers) and heterotrophs (micro- and macroconsumers) linked together in food chains and food webs. Decomposers play the vital role in reducing complex organic matter to inorganic matter and returning nutrients to the environment.

Both abiotic and biotic factors affect the structure of an ecosystem. Limiting factors, such as temperature, light, and available nutrients, are abiotic regulators. They and other abiotic regulators form a complex set of interactions that limit the activities of individual organisms, populations, and communities. Too little, or too much, of a particular limiting factor may affect the organisms that are found in a specific habitat, the area where a species is found. Organisms, populations, and communities have a range of tolerances for each of the limiting factors, a concept known as the law of tolerances. Some organisms have a wide range of tolerances for a limiting factor, such as the concentration of dissolved oxygen in a stream, while others have a very narrow range for that same factor.

Species whose activities determine the structure of the community are called keystone species. Scientists are just beginning to understand the various ways in which members of the biota affect ecosystem structure.

Key Terms

abiota

atom

autotroph

biome

biosphere

biota

carnivore

chemotroph

community

compound

cultural eutrophication

decomposer

detritus feeder

detritivore

ecosystem

element

energy

entropy

eutrophication

first law of energy (first law of thermodynamics)

habitat

herbivore

heterotroph

individual

isotope

keystone species

law of the conservation of matter

law of tolerances

limiting factor

macroconsumer

macronutrient

matter

microconsumer

micronutrient

molecule

omnivore

organic compound

phototroph

population

predator

prey

primary consumer

range of tolerances

scavenger

second law of energy (second law of thermodynamics)

secondary consumer

species

tertiary consumer

Environmental Success Story

Concerned about the use of disposables on their campus, a group of students from James Madison University decided to sell mugs to be used instead. They planned to make others more aware, but it also turned out to be a successful fundraiser. The shipment of 1,000 mugs that they received was gone within two days. After realizing the popularity and profitability of the mugs, the school food service joined in and supported the project--7,500 mugs were sold to a student population of around 10,000. Now the university includes the mugs in the orientation package for first-year students.

True/False

1. A community is an area characterized by a dominant   T   F
   vegetation type.

2. An ecosystem is self-sustaining because it is a completely   T   F
   closed system.

3. Abiotic components of an ecosystem include chemotrophs,   T   F
   detritivores, and decomposers.

4. Heterotrophs obtain energy from autotrophs.   T   F

5. The earth is an open system because it receives energy from the   T   F
   sun.

Fill in the Blank

1. The physical environment in which an organism lives is its _____ .

2. The two components of ecosystems are the _____ and the _____.

3. Molecules made up of two or more elements are known as _____.

4. Chemicals needed by organisms in relatively large quantities for the construction of
   proteins, fats, and carbohydrates are called _____ .

5. Organisms such as grasshoppers and deer, which eat only plants, are
   _____ or _____ .

6. Earthworms and shrimp, which live off the decaying fragments of other organisms,
   are examples of _____ or _____ .

Multiple Choice

Choose the best answer.

1. The region of the eastern U.S. characterized by temperate deciduous forest is an
   example of a(n)
   A. ecosystem
   B. biome
   C. community
   D. abiotic component

2. The amount of energy from the sun reaching the earth each day that is captured through photosynthesis is _____ of the total.
   A. 5–10%
   B. 2–5%
   C. 1–2%
   D. less than 1%

3. Decomposers play a major role in an ecosystem by
   A. reducing complex organic matter to inorganic matter.
   B. returning nutrients to a form which can be used by producers.
   C. contributing to the build-up of nutrients in soil.
   D. All of the above are true.

4. The law which states that during a physical or chemical change energy is neither created nor destroyed is the
   A. first law of energy.
   B. second law of energy.
   C. law of the minimum.
   D. law of tolerances.

5. Atoms of the same element sometimes have different numbers of
   A. protons.
   B. neutrons.
   C. electrons.
   D. molecules.

Short Answer

1. List the seven levels at which ecology is studied.

2. What is entropy?

3. What is an isotope?

4. What are the six macronutrients?

5. What is cultural eutrophication?

Thought Questions

Develop a complete answer for each of the following.

1. How do the biota and abiota interact to regulate the structure of ecosystems?

2. How do limiting factors affect the structure of an ecosystem? Use examples from Environmental Science in Action: Lake Erie in your answer.

3. Explain the roles of producers, consumers, and decomposers in an ecosystem.

Related Concepts

Describe the relationship. (There may be more than one.)

BETWEEN...	AND...
heterotrophs	herbivores
chemotrophs	autotrophs
limiting factors	eutrophication
chemical fertilizers	limiting factors
predators	keystone species

Did You Know . . . ?

A single river in Brazil harbors more species of fish than all the rivers in the United States.

Suggested Activities

1. Observe a terrestrial or aquatic ecosystem first-hand for a few weeks. Identify the autotrophs, primary consumers, secondary consumers, detritus feeders, and microconsumers that make up the food web of the ecosystem. Describe the interactions among them.

2. Study an aquatic ecosystem (pond, lake, stream, river). How is it being used by humans? How have these uses affected its ecological health?

3. Research the demise of dinosaurs. Identify the different limiting factors which have been hypothesized.

CHAPTER 4

Ecosystem Function

Chapter Outline

I. How Do Autotrophs Capture and Use Energy?

    A. Two Types of Autotrophs

        1. Phototrophs

        2. Chemotrophs

    B. Phototrophs

        1. Convert Light Energy to Chemical Energy via Photosynthesis

        2. Contain Chlorophyll

        3. Produce Energy that is the Most Important Driving Force for the Biota

    C. Chemotrophs

        1. Produce Energy from Chemicals Available in the Environment

        2. Represented by Bacteria that Live in Deep Waters or Mud

    D. Measures of Autrophic Energy

        1. Gross Primary Productivity (GPP)

            a. Total Amount of Energy Produced by Autotrophs Over Time

            b. Energy that Can Be Used by Producers Themselves

        2. Net Primary Productivity (NPP)

            a. Amount of Energy Available for Storage after Respiration by

Producers

    b. Amount of Energy Available for Primary Consumers

II. How Does Energy Flow Through a Community?

  A. Food Chain

    1. Community of Organisms Formed by Trophic Levels

    2. First Trophic Level -- Producers

    3. Second Trophic Level -- Primary Consumers (Herbivores)

    4. Third Trophic Level -- Secondary Consumers (Carnivores)

    5. Fourth Trophic Level -- Tertiary Consumers

    6. Decomposers (Microconsumers) Operate at Each Trophic Level

  B. Food Web

    1. Interlocking Food Chains

    2. Defines Feeding Relationships, Movement of Energy/Materials

III. How Does Energy Flow Affect the Structure of an Ecosystem?

  A. Pyramid of Energy

    1. Production, Use, Transfer of Energy Between Trophic Levels

    2. 10 Percent Rule

      a. Applied to Consumption of Organisms at One Trophic Level by Organisms at Another Level

      b. In General, 90% of Available Energy Lost as Heat

      c. Only 10% of Available Energy Transferred at Each Step

  B. Pyramid of Biomass

    1. Depicts the Total Amount of Living Material at Each Level

    2. Total Biomass Tends to Become Smaller at Each Level

    3. Size of Each Individual Tends to Become Larger

C. Pyramid of Numbers

    1. Depicts Relative Abundance of Organisms at Each Trophic Level

    2. In General, Organisms at Lower Levels Are Found in Greater Numbers than Organisms at Higher Levels. For Example, Herbivores Appear in Larger Numbers than Carnivores.

IV. How Do Materials Cycle Through an Ecosystem?

A. Biogeochemical Cycling

    1. Cycling Involves Biological, Geologic, and Chemical Factors

    2. Grouped Into Three Categories

        a. Hydrologic

        b. Gaseous

        c. Sedimentary

B. Hydrologic Cycle

    1. Cycling of Water from Hydrosphere to Atmosphere and Return

    2. Quality and Availability of Water are Variable

C. Gaseous Cycle

    1. Basically Occur in Atmosphere

    2. Most Significant Cycles Include:

        a. Carbon Cycle

        b. Oxygen Cycle

        c. Nitrogen Cycle

D. Sedimentary Cycle

1. Involves Materials that Move from Land to Oceans and Back

2. Most Significant Cycles Include:

    a. Phosphorous Cycle

    b. Sulfur Cycle

Learning Objectives

After learning the material in Chapter 4 you should be able to:

1. Understand how plants capture and use the sun's energy.

2. Define energy, its source, and its various natural laws.

3. Trace the flow of energy through a community.

4. Define trophic levels, food chains, and food webs.

5. Determine how energy flow affects the structure of an ecosystem.

6. Understand the various ways by which materials cycle through an ecosystem.

7. Appreciate the regional, national, and international importance of the Chesapeake Bay resource.

8. Examine the physical, biological, and social characteristics that make the Chesapeake Bay a valuable resource.

9. Recognize the environmental problems associated with an increase in the Bay area's population.

10. Understand both the history of Chesapeake Bay's environmental dilemmas, as well as future management plans designed to prevent the reappearance of such problems.

Did You Know. . . ?

Four species become extinct every second.

Key Concepts

Read this summary of Chapter 4 and identify the important concepts discussed in the chapter.

The biotic and abiotic components of the biosphere are inseparable, bound together by a complex and delicately balanced web of biological and physical processes that regulate the flow of energy and the cycling of materials. Ecosystems constantly receive energy from the sun, which is the lifeblood that fuels the earth's biomass.

Photosynthesis is the process by which phototrophs (producers) capture and convert the sun's light energy to chemical energy. Phototrophs contain chlorophyll, a green pigment which absorbs the light energy that fuels photosynthesis. Using carbon dioxide, water, and light energy, phototrophs produce carbohydrates and lipids; the sun's light energy is transferred to the carbon bonds that form carbohydrates and oxygen is given off. The release of energy from fuel molecules (carbohydrates and lipids) is called respiration. All organisms respire, but only phototrophs can carry out photosynthesis. Only a very small percentage of the energy input from the sun -- 0.023 percent -- is actually captured by phototrophs through photosynthesis, yet that small fraction results in billions of tons of living matter, or biomass.

The gross primary productivity is the total amount of energy produced by autotrophs over a given period of time. The amount of energy available for storage after the producer's own needs are met (through respiration) is the net primary productivity.

Food chains and food webs represent the feeding relationships and the movement of energy and materials among the organisms of the biotic community. In every ecosystem, some consumers feed solely upon producers, while others feed upon both producers and consumers, and still others feed only upon other consumers. The producers and different kinds of consumers are said to occupy different trophic, or feeding, levels. Producers occupy the first trophic level; primary consumers or herbivores (plant eaters) occupy the second; secondary consumers or omnivores (plant and meat eaters) occupy the third; and tertiary consumers or carnivores (meat eaters) occupy the fourth. A food chain is a simplified illustration of the way in which energy and materials move through an ecosystem. That movement is more accurately depicted by food webs, interlocking chains woven into complex associations.

The flow of energy determines trophic relationships and thus affects the structure of the ecosystem. The pyramid of energy represents the production, use, and transfer of energy from one trophic level to another. Generally, only about 10 percent of the available energy is transferred to the next successive trophic level; the rest is lost to the environment as low-quality heat. The pyramid of biomass represents the total amount of living material at each trophic level, and the pyramid of numbers depicts the relative abundance of organisms at each trophic level. In general, lower levels contain a greater number of organisms than successive levels.

Unlike energy, materials cycle through ecosystems and are used over and over again by the biotic community. The processes by which materials cycle involve living organisms as well as geologic and chemical processes. For this reason, they are known as biogeochemical cycles. The hydrologic cycle accounts for the movement and cycling of water from the hydrosphere and lithosphere to the atmosphere and back to the hydrosphere and lithosphere. Gaseous cycles, which take place primarily in the atmosphere, include the carbon, oxygen, and nitrogen cycles. Sedimentary cycles, which involve materials that move chiefly from the lithosphere to the hydrosphere and back to the lithosphere, include phosphorous and sulfur.

Key Terms

biogeochemical cycle

biomass

carbon cycle

detritus food web

food chain

food web

gaseous cycle

gross primary productivity (GPP)

hydrologic cycle

net primary productivity (NPP)

nitrogen cycle

nitrogen fixation

oxygen cycle

phosphorus cycle

photosynthesis

phytoplankton

pyramid of biomass

pyramid of energy

pyramid of numbers

respiration

sedimentary cycle

sulfur cycle

ten (10) percent rule

trophic level

Environmental Success Story

Heading a tree-planting campaign when in college gave Andy Lipkis the idea of starting up a nonprofit organization in Los Angeles called TreePeople. This group trains citizen foresters and educates the public about local and global issues involving forests. Besides educating people, the main activity TreePeople does is plant trees, and it has been very successful in the past decade. Five million trees were planted in Los Angeles, 20 million planted in California, and 100 million planted through the country in order to offset heat islands in cities. Lipkis' philosophy includes the idea that the tree is "a meeting ground for everybody, no matter what their background. Everybody can plant and care for a tree."

True/False

1. Only 0.023% of the sun's energy generates the hundreds of   T   F
   millions of tons of biomass on earth.

2. All autotrophs use sunlight and chlorophyll to produce energy.   T   F

3. Human-made sources contribute more sulfur to the atmosphere T   F
   than natural sources such as volcanoes.

4. Energy cycles and materials flow through ecosystems.   T   F

5. In general, higher trophic levels represent a greater amount of   T   F
    stored energy, a greater amount of biomass, and a greater
    number of organisms than do lower levels.

Fill in the Blank

1. The microscopic organisms that capture and store most of the energy in aquatic
    habitats are _____.

2. The process in which energy from fuel (food) is released is _____.

3. _____ is the process by which some kinds of bacteria convert free
    nitrogen to nitrates or ammonium.

4. The most significant gaseous cycles are the _____ , _____ ,
    and _____ cycles.

5. An increase in atmospheric CO_2 may cause a climatic change known as

    _____ .

Multiple Choice

Choose the best answer.

1. Of the approximately 1.5 million $kcal/m^2/yr$ which reach the earth from the sun,
    about 34%
    A. is reflected back to space.
    B. is absorbed by the biosphere.
    C. heats the land and warms the atmosphere.
    D. generates wind currents.

2. Nitrogen is converted to a usable form by
    A. bacteria living in the soil or in plant roots.
    B. lightning.
    C. decomposers during respiration.
    D. All of the above are true.

3. The nutrient that is a major structural component of shells, bones, and teeth is
   A. oxygen.
   B. ammonium.
   C. phosphorus.
   D. nitrogen.

4. The most common element in living tissue is
   a. carbon.
   b. nitrogen.
   c. oxygen.
   d. hydrogen.

Short Answer

1. What is respiration?

2. What is the pyramid of energy?

3. What is the pyramid of numbers?

4. What is the pyramid of biomass?

5. How does the biosphere recycle the carbon dioxide that is produced by processes such as respiration and combustion of fossil fuels?

Thought Questions

Develop a complete answer for each of the following.

1. How does the sun's energy become the food on which we live? What happens to the energy that reaches earth's atmosphere? How do green plants convert it to stored energy?

2. Which ecosystems are the most productive (efficient at producing energy)? Why? Compare these to less productive ecosystems.

3. Why is food web a more accurate term than food chain? Why is a detritus food web a particularly good example of this? Why are there usually no more than three or four trophic levels in a given ecosystem?

4. Explain the implications of the 10 percent rule for human diets. How does the typical diet in the U.S. compare with the typical diet in China?

5. Describe the major biogeochemical cycles. What happens when the cycling is interrupted in some way? Use examples from Environmental Science in Action: The Chesapeake Bay.

Related Concepts

Describe the relationship. (There may be more than one.)

BETWEEN...	AND...
photosynthesis	chemosynthesis
10% rule	pyramid of energy
net primary productivity	gross primary productivity

Did You Know...?

Since 1960, 200 percent more garbage has been generated due to the increase in packaging.

Suggested Activities

1. Take note of the food you eat during the next week. At what trophic level do you normally eat? How might you change your eating habits to be more energy efficient?

2. What is your role in biogeochemical cycling? Try to identify all the things you do that move materials through the cycle. For example, if you wash your laundry with a detergent containing phosphates, you are cycling phosphorus. By driving to class you are releasing CO_2 and nitrous oxides (among other things) into the air.

3. Eat less meat. Prepare meals from fruits, vegetables, and grains.

CHAPTER 5

Ecosystem Development and Dynamic Equilibrium

Chapter Outline

I. What Causes Ecosystems to Change?

    A. Natural Forces

    B. Human Activity

II. How Do Ecosystems Develop?

    A. Development Via Succession

        1. Process By Which an Ecosystem Matures

        2. Progresses to Climax Community

            a. Organisms Best Adapted for Conditions in Defined Area

            b. Usually Dominated by a Few Abundant Plant Species

        3. Occurs in Both Aquatic and Terrestrial Environments

    B. Primary Succession

        1. Development of Ecosystem in Area Once Devoid of Organisms

        2. Stages Consist of:

            a. Lichen Pioneer Community

            b. Moss Community

            c. Herbaceous Community

            d. Shrub Community

e. Tree Community

f. Climax Forest or Equilibrium Community

C. Secondary Succession

1. Changes that Occur After an Ecosystem Has Been Disturbed

2. Disturbances Usually a Result of Human Activity

3. Stages Include:

a. Annual Weed Community

b. Perennial Weed Community

1. Goldenrods as Example

2. Food Source for a Variety of Insects

3. Galls Protect Insect Eggs

4. Supports Rich Diversity of Life

c. Shrub or Young Tree Community

d. Young Forest Community

e. Climax Forest Community

D. Ecotone

1. Area Where Different Communities Meet

2. Stages of Succession Blend

3. Zone of Transition and Intense Competition

4. Regions Supporting Great Diversity of Life

E. Succession in Ponds, Lakes and Wetlands

1. Maturation of Lake or Pond, Caused by Nutrient Enrichment, is Known as Eutrophication

2. Usually Proceeds to Terrestrial Climax

3. Nutrient Enrichment, and Thus Eutrophication, May Be Caused By Natural Factors or Human Activity

4. As In the Everglades, Marshes Can Be a Climax Community

III. What Is Dynamic Equilibrium?

A. Climax Communities Undergo Constant Change

B. "Stability" of Ecosystem Based on Continued Reaction to Change

IV. What Factors Contribute to Dynamic Equilibrium?

A. Feedback

1. Maintained by System of Checks and Balances

2. Positive Feedback -- Continues a Particular Trend

3. Negative Feedback -- Reverses a Particular Trend

B. Species Interactions

1. Competition

a. Occurs When Two or More Individuals Vie for Resources

b. Intraspecific -- Between Members of the Same Species

c. Interspecific -- Between Members of Different Species

2. Cooperation

a. Intraspecific -- Social Structure of Bees, Ants

b. Interspecific -- Mutualism, Commensalism, Parasitism

3. Predation

C. Nonhuman Population Dynamics

1. Five Phases of Population Growth

a. Lag Phase

b. Slow Growth

c. Log (Exponential) Growth

d. Equilibrium

e. Decline

2. Biotic Potential

a. Maximum Growth Rate a Population Can Achieve

b. Limited by Factors Known as Environmental Resistance

3. Two Types of Environmental Resistance

a. Density-dependent, or Biotic

b. Density-independent, or Abiotic

D. Species Diversity

1. Complex Relations Between Diversity and Dynamic Equilibrium

2. Illustrates Lack of Understanding of Ecosystem Relationships

Learning Objectives

After learning the material in Chapter 5 you should be able to:

1. Identify the causes of environmental change.

2. List and understand the stages involved in primary/secondary succession.

3. Identify the diversity of organisms supported by goldenrod fields.

4. Appreciate the paradox of stable communities maintaining dynamic equilibrium.

5. Briefly summarize the "Gaia" hypothesis.

6. List and understand the factors contributing to the dynamic equilibrium of an ecosystem.

7. Become aware of the various means through which ecosystems seek to restore stability.

8. Recognize the different ways in which species interact.

9. Define the five phases of nonhuman population dynamics.

10. Appreciate the regional, national, and international importance of the Everglades as a resource.

11. List the indispensable functions that a healthy Everglades ecosystem performs.

12. Identify the various human/wildlife uses of the Everglades region.

13. Understand both the history of dealing with the Everglades' environmental dilemmas and future management plans designed to prevent the reappearance of such problems.

14. Identify Marjory Stoneman Douglas, and describe how her work has affected the Everglades.

Did You Know. . . ?

One hundred percent of United States oil use could be replaced by the natural gas emitted from garbage dumps and rotting vegetation.

Key Concepts

Read this summary of Chapter 5 and identify the important concepts discussed in the chapter.

Nature is not static; all ecosystems change and all undergo ecological succession, the gradual, sequential, and somewhat predictable change in the composition of the biotic community. This maturation process is also known as ecosystem development, a term that accounts for the accompanying modifications in the physical environment. Primary succession is the development of a community in an area previously devoid of organisms; opportunistic species known as pioneer organisms invade the area and colonize it. Secondary succession is the change in community types after an area has been disturbed, generally by human activity. Successional stages are not discrete; they tend to blend into one another. For any defined geographic area, as succession proceeds, the species composition of the community changes until the association of organisms best suited to the physical conditions of that area is reached. This association of organisms is known as the climax community.

Ecosystems continually react to change and disturbance, thereby maintaining a dynamic equilibrium, or dynamic steady state. Ecosystems maintain a dynamic equilibrium either by resisting change (inertia) or by restoring structure and function after a disturbance (resilience). Three factors that enable the ecosystem to maintain dynamic equilibrium are feedback, species interactions, and population dynamics. Positive feedback continues a particular trend, and can be disruptive, while negative feedback reverses a trend, and therefore tends to stabilize the system. Species interactions include predator-prey relationships, competition, and cooperation. Competition and cooperation can take place between individuals of the same species or between individuals of different species. When two species occupy similar ecological niches -- defined as an organism's functional role within the community -- interspecific competition becomes particularly keen. Situations in which interspecific competition leads to the exclusion or (local) extinction of one of the species illustrate the principle of competitive exclusion. Interspecific cooperation includes symbiosis, the intimate association of two dissimilar species regardless of the benefits or lack of benefits to both species. Mutualism is a symbiotic relationship in which both species benefit. An association in which one species benefits and the other neither benefits nor is harmed is an example of commensalism. Parasitism occurs when one species benefits and the other is harmed.

Population dynamics also contribute to ecosystem stability. In laboratory studies scientists have found that populations of organisms commonly exhibit five phases of growth. In contrast, natural populations fluctuate over time around the carrying capacity of the environment, the number of individuals the environment or habitat can best support. Limiting factors, collectively known as environmental resistance, prevent a population from realizing its biotic potential, that is, the maximum growth rate the population could achieve given unlimited resources and ideal environmental conditions. Environmental resistance factors may be density-dependent (effect is greater when the population density is high) or density-independent (population density does not play a role; density-independent factors set upper limits on the population).

Key Terms

biotic potential

carrying capacity

climax community

commensalism

competition

competitive exclusion principle

cooperation

density-dependent factor

density-independent factor

dynamic equilibrium

dynamic steady state

ecosystem development

ecosystem succession

ecotone

ectoparasite

endoparasite

environmental resistance

eutrophication

generalist niche

host

inertia

interspecific competition

interspecific cooperation

intraspecific competition

intraspecific cooperation

mutualism

negative feedback

niche

opportunistic species

parasite

parasitism

pioneer organism

positive feedback

predation

primary succession

resiliency

secondary succession

specialist niche

stress

symbiosis

Environmental Success Story

In order to save money on hauling fees, the Hyatt Regency in Chicago has recently set up a recycling center. The over 2,000-room hotel had an annual waste stream of 7 million pounds, but this is being combated by the employees, who are equipped with special receptacles for the recoverable waste. In the first five months of operation, 250,000 pounds of cardboard, paper, glass, and aluminum cans were saved for recycling. Considering that the hotel expects to save $100,000 on annual hauling fees and bring in another $20,000 selling the recyclables, the $25,000 recycling center will more than pay for itself.

True/False

1. In a climax community, production equals respiration. T F

2. Ecotones have greater diversity than the adjacent habitats. T F

3. The climax community of aquatic ecosystems is always a marsh T F
   or swamp community.

4. In general, negative feedback is destabilizing to an ecosystem. T F

5. Density-independent factors tend to set upper limits on T F
   population size.

Fill in the Blank

1. The process by which an ecosystem matures is _____.

2. The ability of a natural system to resist change is known as _____.

3. An _____ is an organism that lives in the body cavity, organs or
   blood or another organism, causing it harm.

4. The first phase of population growth in a controlled environment, in which the
   population does not grow, is called the _____.

5. An environment's_____ is the population size it can
   best sustain.

Multiple Choice

Choose the best answer.

1. The zone of transition and intense competition where different communities meet is
   a(n)
   A. ecotone.
   B. pioneer community.
   C. biome.
   D. niche.

2. Two species competing for the same habitat in a community is an example of a(n)
   A. specialist niche.
   B. intraspecific competition.
   C. interspecific competition.
   D. competitive exclusion principle.

3. In controlled lab environments, animal populations pass through phases. The first three phases are
   A. lag, exponential growth, slow growth.
   B. lag, dynamic equilibrium, exponential growth.
   C. slow growth, exponential growth, dynamic equilibrium.
   D. lag, slow growth, exponential growth.

4. An example of mutualism is
   A. remora fish that attach to sharks.
   B. liver flukes in cattle.
   C. ticks on sheep.
   D. lichens.

5. Symbiosis is when two species interact and
   A. one is harmed and the other benefited.
   B. both are either harmed or benefited.
   C. one is benefited, the other is neither harmed nor benefited.
   D. both are benefited.

Short Answer

1. What is stress?

2. What is a climax community?

3. What is the difference between primary and secondary succession?

4. What is the role of pioneer organisms in ecosystem development?

5. What is the competitive exclusion principle?

Thought Questions

Develop a complete answer for each of the following.

1. Describe the primary succession from bare rock to climax forest. What determines the dominant species in the climax community? What stops a climax community from further succession?

2. How does dynamic equilibrium relate to the concept of the "balance of nature?"

3. How do feedback, species interactions, and population dynamics contribute to the dynamic equilibrium of ecosystems?

4. Why is interspecific competition most intense when two different species occupy similar ecological niches?

5. Why do natural populations never reach their biotic potential?

Related Concepts

Describe the relationship. (There may be more than one.)

BETWEEN...	AND...
niche	habitat
diversity	ecosystem stability
specialist niche	generalist niche
density-dependent factor	density-independent factor
pioneer species	climax community

Did You Know...?

It would take only one year to make enough plastic film to shrink-wrap the state of Texas.

Suggested Activities

1. Observe an old field or other disturbed area for evidence of succession activity. What species do you find there? What stage of succession is occurring?

2. Locate an ecotone. Which species are competing with one another? Can you identify any transitional species?

CHAPTER 6

Ecosystem Degradation

Chapter Outline

I.   What Is Ecosystem Damage?

    A. Adverse Alteration of System's Integrity, Diversity, Productivity

    B. Pollutants as Major Cause

    C. Five Factors Determining the Extent of Damage:

        1. Quantity of Pollutant

        2. Persistence of Pollutant

        3. How Pollutant Enters the Environment

            a. Point Source -- Identifiable, Specific Source

            b. Nonpoint Source -- From Wide Area, Hard to Control

            c. Cross-media -- Move from One Medium (Air, Water, Soil) to Next

        4. Effect of Pollutant

            a. Acute -- Effects Occur Immediately, Easily Detectable

            b. Chronic -- Long-term Effects, Unnoticed for Years

            c. Bioaccumulation -- Storage of Chemicals in an Organism in Higher Concentrations than are Normally Found in the Environment

            d. Biomagnification -- Accumulation of Chemicals in Organisms in Increasingly Higher Concentrations at Successive Trophic Levels

5. Time It Takes to Remove Pollutant

II. What Is Ecosystem Disruption?

A. Rapid Change in Species Composition Traced Directly to Human Acts

B. Disruption As a Result of:

1. Persistent Pesticides

2. Introduction of New (Exotic) Species

3. Construction

4. Overexploitation of Resources

III. What Is Ecosystem Destruction?

A. Replacement of a Natural System by a Human System

B. Major Causes Include:

1. Urbanization

2. Transportation

3. Agriculture

IV. What Is Desertification?

A. Expansion Into/Creation of Desert Conditions in Areas Where Those Conditions Do Not Normally Occur

B. Often the Result of:

1. Overgrazing

2. Overcultivation

3. Deforestation

4. Poor Irrigation Practices

V. What Is Deforestation?

    A. Cutting Down and Clearing Away of Forests

    B. Results in Erosion, Loss of Native Forest Species

    C. Tropical Rain Forests

        1. Home to 3-30 Million Species of Plants and Animals

        2. Moderate Temperatures of Entire Planet

        3. Deforestation as a Result of Political, Social, and Economic Factors

    D. Ancient Forests of the Pacific Northwest and Alaska

        1. Home to Very Old, Very Large Trees

        2. Logging Community Increasing Pressure to Harvest

        3. Home of the Endangered/Protected Northern Spotted Owl

Learning Objectives

After learning the materials in Chapter 6 you should be able to:

1. Recognize that human activity that alters environmental conditions degrades the environment in some way.

2. List and understand "the 5 D's" associated with human activity and degradation.

3. Identify the five major factors which determine how pollutants damage natural systems.

4. Define and give an example of a "persistent pollutant."

5. Differentiate between point and non-point pollutants and give several examples of each.

6. Differentiate between acute and chronic effects of pollutants.

7. Define synergistic effect, bioaccumulation, and biomagnification.

8. Recognize the disruptive consequences which result from: changing species composition, impeding species movement, and exploiting an ecosystem's resources.

9. Identify the three human activities most often associated with the destruction of a natural system.

10. Become familiar with the economic factors which have contributed to the sharp increase of desertification and deforestation practices, and the subsequent adverse environmental results.

11. Examine the blue, gray, and humpback whales' physical, biological, and social boundaries.

12. Understand the human history of dealing with whale species and future management plans.

Did You Know. . . ?

Between 60-80 percent of all live wild animals smuggled around the world die in transit.

Key Concepts

Read this summary of Chapter 6 and identify the important concepts discussed in the chapter.

Ecosystems become degraded when human activities alter environmental conditions in such a way that they exceed the range of tolerances for one or more organisms in the biotic community. A degraded ecosystem loses some capacity to support the diversity of life forms that are best suited to its particular physical environment. The five D's of ecosystem degradation are damage, disruption, destruction, desertification, and deforestation.

Damage occurs when the integrity of natural systems is altered. A pollutant is a substance or form of energy, such as heat, that adversely alters the physical, chemical, or biological quality of natural systems or that accumulates in living organisms in amounts that threaten their health or survival. Five factors determine the damage done by pollutants: the quantity of the pollutant discharged to the environment, the persistence of the pollutant, the way in which the pollutant enters the environment, the effect of the pollutant, and the time it takes the ecosystem to remove the pollutant.

A rapid change in the species composition of a community that can be traced directly to a specific human activity is known as a disruption. Activities that may lead to a change in species composition are the use of persistent pesticides, the introduction of new species into an area (usually accidental), the construction of dams or highways, and the overexploitation of resources.

A more common form of natural system degradation is ecosystem destruction. A natural system is destroyed when it is replaced by a human system. Perhaps the most serious consequences of natural system destruction are habitat loss and the loss of the functions and services provided by natural systems, functions that human systems cannot duplicate.

Two specific types of natural system degradation are desertification, the expansion into or creation of desertlike conditions in areas where such conditions do not usually occur, and deforestation, the cutting down or clearing of forests. Overgrazing, overcultivation, deforestation, and poor irrigation practices are the major causes of desertification. Conversion to farmland and pastureland; the demand for fuel, timber, and paper products; and the construction of roadways are the major causes of deforestation. Both desertification and deforestation are increasing at alarming rates.

Key Terms

acute effect

bioaccumulation

biodegradable

biomagnification

chronic effect

cross-media pollutant

nonbiodegradable

nonpoint source

persistent pollutant

point source

pollutant

riparian zone

siltation

synergistic effect

Environmental Success Story

When Dale Shields noticed a brown pelican on a rock while fishing one summer day, he thought it was dead. Fortunately, he went closer and found that it was still alive. He called around the Sarasota, Florida area that he calls home, but no one could help him. He then took the bird into his own care and it survived. This was just the beginning of a decade of rescuing and rehabilitating birds. In 1985, Shields founded the Protect Our Pelicans Society, which now has more than 4,000 members. A pelican in the Sarasota Bay is expected to live only seven years, compared with the normal life expectancy of around 30 years. One cause of this is uninformed fishermen. When a pelican becomes entangled in a fishing line, most fishermen just cut the line instead of reeling it in and removing the hook. Because of this, some birds, when returning to their roosts, become entangled in the line and hang themselves. Thanks to Dale Shields and his group, over 3,000 pelicans have been freed from the life-threatening fishing line.

True/False

1. Persistent pollutants can be both biodegradable and nonbiodegradable.   T   F

2. The primary cause of species extinction is habitat loss.   T   F

3. Though expensive, it is usually possible to rehabilitate ecosystems that have undergone desertification.   T   F

4. Worldwide, the most common cause of deforestation is the demand for timber and paper products.   T   F

5. DDT is an example of a persistent pollutant.   T   F

Fill in the Blank

1. The Five D's of Natural System Degradation are_____, _____ ,_____, _, and _____..

2. A(n) _____ is a rapid change in the species composition of a community that can be traced directly to a specific human activity.

3. _____ occurs when a living system is replaced by a human system.

4. A smokestack that releases pollutants into the environment is a(n) _____ source.

5. A pollutant which can move from one type of environment (e.g., air) to another (e.g., water) is a _____.

Multiple Choice

Choose the best answer.

1. All of the following are example of cross-media pollution except
   A. landfill leachate.
   B. photochemical smog.
   C. acid precipitation.
   D. groundwater contamination.

2. All of the following are examples of destruction except
   A. conversion of grassland to cropland.
   B. draining of coastal wetlands for agricultural use.
   C. conversion of cropland to housing developments.
   D. None of the above is true.

3. Substances that enter a system in a form unusable by organisms in that system are called
   A. nonbiodegradable.
   B. biodegradable.
   C. persistent.
   D. acute.

4. When a chemical is stored in an organism in higher concentrations than are normally found in the environment, it is an example of
   A. biomagnification.
   B. bioaccumulation.
   C. persistent pollutants.
   D. synergism.

5. Worldwide, the primary cause of deforestation is
   A. logging and the paper products industry
   B. urban sprawl.
   C. the construction of roadways.
   D. conversion to agricultural land.

Short Answer

1. What five factors determine how a pollutant affects the environment?

2. What is synergism? Give an example.

3. What types of ecosystems are most susceptible to desertification and why?

4. What are the major causes of deforestation?

5. What is lag time?

Thought Questions

Develop a complete answer for each of the following.

1. Describe the five types of natural system degradation and give examples of each. Discuss how their major causes are interrelated.

2. Explain why nonpoint source pollution is difficult to measure or control.

3. Explain bioaccumulation and biomagnification. How do trophic levels relate to biomagnification?

4. Discuss the damage caused by the use of persistent pesticides, and explain how resistant populations develop.

5. What are the benefits of forests and what are the threats of deforestation? Why are tropical rain forests of particular concern?

Related Concepts

Describe the relationship. (There may be more than one.)

BETWEEN...	AND...
irrigation	desertification
persistent pollutant	biomagnification
acute effect	chronic effect
ocean dumping	oxygen depletion
persistent pesticide	resistant populations

> **Did You Know. . . ?**
>
> Americans throw away the equivalent of more than 30 million trees in newsprint each year.

Suggested Activities

1. Identify one or more non-native species in your area. How were they introduced? What impact are they having on the ecosystem?

2. Choose an area of the world that is threatened by desertification or deforestation. Find out more about the causes of the damage, and outline an environmentally sound management plan for the ecosystem, including strategies for eliminating the causes.

3. Track the history of an endangered or extinct species. What kinds of ecosystem damage caused the species' decline?

CHAPTER 7

Applying Ecological Principles

Chapter Outline

I.   What Is Applied Ecology?

    A. Attempts to Predict Ecological Consequences of Human Activity

    B. Recommends Ways to Limit Damage to and Restore Ecosystems

    C. Challenge to Identify and Lessen Effects of Human Activities

    D. Six Subdisciplines

        1. Disturbance Ecology

            a. Predicts Impact of Stress on Natural Systems

            b. Aids In the Formation of Environmental Impact Statements

        2. Restoration Ecology

            a. Repairs Biotic Communities After a Disturbance

            b. Maintains Present Diversity of Species and Ecosystems

            c. Increase Knowledge to Restore/Manage Other Systems

        3. Landscape Ecology

            a. Earth as Patchwork of Individual Ecosystems

            b. Study Ecosystem Distribution, Their Function and Change

            c. Relations between Humans, Living Space Important

        4. Agroecology

            a. Also Known as Agricultural Ecology

            b. Study of Agroecosystems with Long-term Management Goal

c. Emphasis on Protection of the Health of the Soil

5. Conservation Ecology

    a. Also Known as Preservation Ecology

    b. Application of Ecological Principles to Conserve Species

    c. Focus On:

        1. Protecting Habitat

        2. Mitigating the Harmful Effects of Human Activities

        3. Use of Less Intrusive Management Techniques

    d. Conservation: Management of Area for its Continued Use

    e. Preservation: Human Use Restricted; Strict Conservation

6. Ecological Toxicology

    a. Also Known as Ecotoxicology

    b. Study of the Effect of Toxins on Ecosystems

    c. Attempts to Understand, Predict, Monitor Toxin Effects

    d. Goal: Suggestions for Mitigating Pollution's Effects

II. How Can Computer Models Help Applied Ecologists?

A. Models Simulate Ecosystem Structure, Function, and Change

B. Models Aid Applied Ecologists in Several Ways:

1. Predict Ecosystem Response to Stress

2. Predict the Effect of Management Strategies on Ecosystems

3. Understand How Ecosystems Maintain a Dynamic Steady State

Learning Objectives

After learning the material in Chapter 7 you should be able to:

1. Become acquainted with the idea that environmental management is equated to managing human impact.

2. Describe the discipline of applied ecology and its associated challenges.

3. Identify, describe, and differentiate between the six subdisciplines of applied ecology.

4. Explain the importance of computer modeling to applied ecology; describe its advantages and disadvantages.

5. Understand how knowledge of applied ecology can aid in environmental problem solving and ecosystem management.

6. Describe a prairie ecosystem and identify the various characteristics that make it unique.

7. Explain the role of fire in a prairie ecosystem.

8. Identify Fermi National Accelerator Laboratory, its variety of scientific operations, and the management plans and goals incorporated into maintaining the prairie on its grounds.

Did You Know. . . ?

The U.S. Army estimates it will take 1.5 million garbage bags per month to clean up war-torn Kuwait.

Key Concepts

Read this summary of Chapter 7 and identify the important concepts discussed in the chapter.

Six subdisciplines of applied ecology are disturbance ecology, restoration ecology, landscape ecology, agroecology, conservation ecology, and ecotoxicology. Disturbance ecology is primarily concerned with assessing the impact of particular stresses on particular organisms, populations, and ecosystems; understanding the causes and effects of change in natural systems; and planning and designing appropriate projects to mitigate the adverse effects of human activities.

Although closely related to disturbance ecology, restoration ecology is a distinct subdiscipline that is driven largely by the values of society. Its three main goals are to repair biotic communities after a disturbance, to reestablish them on the original site if possible or on other sites if the original sites can no longer be used; to maintain the present diversity of species and ecosystems by finding ways to preserve biotic communities or to protect them from human disturbance so that they can evolve naturally; and 3) to increase knowledge of biotic communities and restoration techniques that can be applied to restore or maintain a particular species or ecosystem. The construction of reefs and the use of fire are important management techniques for restoration ecologists.

Landscape ecology attempts to understand how ecosystems interact to form a larger landscape. It is holistic in its focus on the connections among various subunits, or patches, of the landscape. It is especially interested in the relations between human society and its living space, both the natural and managed components of the landscape.

Agroecology is concerned with developing methods of food production that are ecologically sustainable. Agroecology often incorporates ideas and practices that reflect a sensitivity to social and environmental concerns. Its roots are in the agricultural sciences, ecology, the environmental movement, studies of the agricultural practices and knowledge of indigenous peoples, and studies of rural development.

Conservation ecology is the application of ecological principles and knowledge in order to conserve species and communities. Although there is some overlap between restoration and conservation ecology, they differ in focus and techniques. Restorationists tend to use intrusive management tools to mimic the effects of natural forces which humans have displaced (such as prescribed burns and logging to duplicate the effects of wildfires). Conservation ecologists use less intrusive techniques as they focus on protecting habitat and mitigating the harmful effects of human activities. Examples of such techniques include creating nest and den sites for various birds and mammals or decreasing siltation loading to streams in order to improve fish habitat.

Ecological toxicology is a merger of ecology and toxicology. Ecotoxicologists study, monitor, and predict the consequences of a wide variety of pollutants in order to offer suggestions for mitigating pollution effects.

The various subdisciplines of applied ecology share some common techniques and tools. One of the most common of these is the computer model. Computer models are sophisticated mathematical equations that help ecologists understand how ecosystems respond to stress and to predict the effects of management strategies. Because of the complexity of natural systems, it takes years of careful observation and data collection to develop and accurate computer model.

Key Terms

agroecology

agroecosystem

applied ecology

computer model

conservation

conservation ecology

disturbance ecology

ecotoxicology

landscape

patch

prescribed burning

preservation

restoration ecology

toxicants

toxicology

toxin

Environmental Success Story

A big problem that cattle and pig farmers face in warm weather is the large numbers of houseflies that spread disease. Most farmers spray chemical pesticides, but an alternative method is to use Muscovy ducks to control the flies. Dr. Gordon Surgeoner and Barry Glofcheskie of the University of Guelph in Ontario, Canada conducted an experiment to test the effectiveness of this method. They put a five-week-old Muscovy in an eight cubic foot cage with 400 flies and let it do its work; after just one hour, the duck had consumed 326 flies. When they tried similar experiments outdoors, the ducks trimmed the fly populations by 80 to 90 percent. Unlike most flycatching devices, which must be kept away from animals, some of the ducks even develop a friendly relationship with the farm animals. There are also obvious economic advantages; the chemical control of flies costs over $150 annually for a 35-cow dairy, while a Muscovy duckling costs around two dollars.

True/False

1. One of the goals of restoration ecology is to allow natural   T   F
    succession to occur.

2. The emphasis of agroecology is on protecting the health of the   T   F
    soil.

3. Conservation ecologists try to improve the carrying capacity of   T   F
    ecosystems.

4. Applied ecology is a value-free discipline.   T   F

5. Most toxicological work done to date has focused on the effects   T   F
    of specific substances on organisms rather than on communities
    or ecosystems.

Fill in the Blank

1. The subdiscipline of applied ecology which assesses the impact of stresses on
    organisms, populations, and ecosystems is _____.

2. _____ is the subdiscipline of applied ecology that focuses on the
    relations between human society and its living space.

3. Certain species, called _____, are more sensitive to pollutants than others,
    and are useful in determining when pollutant levels are unsafe.

4. The study of purely ecological phenomena within the crop field is called
_____.

5. The wise use and planned management of an area or resource in order to ensure its continued use is known as _____ , while _____ is the management of an area in ways that restrict its use to nonconsumptive activities.

Multiple Choice

Choose the best answer.

1. The building of artificial reefs is an example of a technique used in
   A. conservation ecology.
   B. restoration ecology.
   C. landscape ecology.
   D. All of the above are true.

2. The ecologist most likely to be involved in developing an environmental impact statement is a(n)
   A. restoration ecologist.
   B. agroecologist.
   C. disturbance ecologist.
   D. preservation ecologist.

3. The primary focus of agroecology is
   A. preserving biological diversity.
   B. protecting the health of the soil.
   C. using integrated pest management.
   D. maximizing the genetic potential of hybrids.

4. Which of the following is not a technique (tool) used by conservation ecologists?
   A. constructing den or nest sites
   B. employing alley cropping
   C. increasing oxygen content in streams
   D. decreasing siltation in streams

5. Which of the following make the development of computer models a difficult and uncertain process?
   A. lack of necessary data to compare stressed and unstressed systems
   B. disagreement over which problems should be addressed
   C. lack of computers powerful enough to process the pertinent data
   D. too few ecologists are interested in developing or using computer models

Short Answer

1. List the six subdisciplines of applied ecology.

2. How does applied ecology differ from ecology?

3. What are the three major goals of restoration ecology?

4. What is conservation ecology?

5. How do agroecosystems differ from natural ecosystems?

Thought Questions

Develop a complete answer for each of the following.

1. Discuss the use of prescribed burning and other techniques to keep ecosystems in certain successional stages. How do societal values play a role in determining which ecosystems are maintained in this way?

2. How is conservation ecology similar to restoration ecology? How is it different?

3. Discuss the use of computer models in applied ecology. What are the benefits of using these models? What are their limitations?

4. Which subdiscipline of applied ecology do you think is most valuable and why?

5. How do social and cultural factors influence each of the 6 subdisciplines of applied ecology? Consider each subdiscipline separately and illustrate your answer with examples.

Related Concepts

Describe the relationship. (There may be more than one.)

BETWEEN...	AND...
conservation	preservation
indicator species	bioaccumulation
jack pines in Michigan	meadows in Yosemite National Park
landscape ecology	satellite imagery
computer models	scientific hypothesis

Did You Know...?

One in four pharmaceuticals comes from a plant native to a tropical rainforest.

Suggested Activities

1. Review an environmental impact statement. What contributions do you think applied ecology made to this document?

2. Visit a restored ecosystem in your area. What is its history? What techniques were used to restore it?

UNIT THREE

AN ENVIRONMENTAL IMPERATIVE

CHAPTER 8

Human Population Dynamics

Chapter Outline

I. Describing the Human Resource: Biological Boundaries

    A. Can the Human Population Be Considered a Resource?

    B. The Great Population Debate

        1. "No Population Problem"

            a. Cornucopians -- people as the world's ultimate resource

            b. Marxists -- poverty result of distribution, not population

        2. "There Is A Population Problem"

            a. Malthusians -- growth greater than earth's sustaining power

            b. Neomalthusians -- continued growth viewed as a threat

            c. Zero Population Growth -- population planning to avert disaster

        3. "The 'Population Problem' Is a Complex Issue"

            a. Problems result of unequal distribution of resources

            b. Over-consumption as environmental problem

    C. What Is Demography?

    D. Why Do We Study Demography?

    E. How Are Populations Measured?

        1. Number of People

a. Absolute Numbers (World) = Total Live Births - Total Deaths

b. Absolute Numbers (Country or Region) = Births + Immigration - Deaths + Emigration

2. Growth Rate

   a. Crude Birth Rate (CBR): Number of Live Births per 1,000 People

   b. Crude Death Rate (CDR): Number of Deaths per 1,000 People

   c. Zero Population Growth (ZPG): Births = Deaths; Zero Growth Rate

3. Regions of Highest Population Increase

   a. Growth Rates are Highest in LDCs

   b. Rapid Population Growth of LDCs Attributed to Improved Medical Care that has Reduced Death Rates, Lack of Access to Family Planning Services and Birth Control, and a High Incidence of Infant Mortality, Which Compels Parents to Have Many Children

4. Population Doubling Time

   a. Determined by Rule of 70:
   70/Current Annual Growth Rate = Doubling Time in Years

   b. LDCs Have the Shortest Doubling Times

5. Factors Affecting Growth Rates

   a. Migration

   b. Fertility, Actual Bearing of Offspring:

      1. General Fertility Rate: Number of Live Births per 1,000 Women of Childbearing Years (Either Ages 15-44 or 15-49)

      2. Age-specific Fertility Rate: Number of Live Births per 1,000 Women of a Specific Age Group per Year

      3. Total Fertility Rate: Average Number of Children a Woman Will Bear Throughout Her Life, Based on the Current Age-Specific Fertility Rate and Assuming Current

Birth Rate Remains Constant Throughout Her Life

    4. Even After Fertility Rates Drop, Large Numbers of Children Ensure Population Momentum and Continued Growth

  c. Age Distribution

    1. Graphically Represented by Population Profile

    2. LCDs with Pyramidal-Shaped Profile; MDCs with More Rectangular or Columnar Profile

    3. Important Indicator of Future Growth Rates

    4. Determines a Nation's Dependency Load, the Proportion of the Population Below 15 or Above 65

6. Population Growth and Economic Development

  a. Every 1% Increase in Population Needs a 3% Increase in GNP

  b. High Growth Rates of LCDs Have Overwhelmed Governments

II. Describing the Human Resource: Physical Boundaries

A. What Can We Learn from Studying Nonhuman Population Dynamics?

  1. The Upper Limit or Maximum Population Size for a Given Area is Determined by the Biological Carrying Capacity of the Environment, the Maximum Number of a Particular Species that the Environment Can Support

  2. Most Populations Fluctuate Around the Optimum Population Size, the Number of Individuals that the Environment Can Best Support

B. Why Do Biologists Calculate the Carrying Capacity of an Environment?

1. Determine the Number of Organisms that Can Be Sustained Over Time

2. Estimates of Carrying Capacity Vary with Weather/Food Fluctuations

3. Wildlife Biologists Use Information to Avoid Population Explosions and Crashes

C. Carrying Capacity as Applied to Human Populations

1. No Standard Carrying Capacity Equation for Humans

2. Humans Classified Geopolitically; Meaningless Terms Ecologically

3. Humans Can Raise Carrying Capacity of Environment with Technology

4. Standards of Living Vary from Region to Region

5. When Standards of Living Dramatically Drop, Environmental Refugees Result

    a. Population Exceeds Carrying Capacity

    b. Environment Degraded

    c. People Abandon Homes Because Land Cannot Support Them

III. Describing the Resource: Social Boundaries

A. What Do Demographic Statistics Tell About Quality of Life?

1. Population Density

    a. How Closely People Are Grouped

    b. Densely Populated Countries often Perceive Problem as One Of Too Little Space rather than Too Large a Population; Such a Perception Can Lead to Expansionist Policies

2. Urbanization

    a. Rise in Number and Size of Cities

    b. High Concentration of People = High Concentrations of Pollution + Waste

3. Life Expectancy at Birth

    a. Average Number of Years a Newborn Can Be Expected to Live

    b. Indicator of Nation's Standard of Living

    c. Low Life Expectancies Attributed to War, Hunger, and Infant and Childhood Mortality

4. Infant and Childhood Mortality

    a. Infant Mortality Rate (IMR): Annual Number of Infants Under Age 1 Who Die per 1,000 Births

    b. IMR is Best Single Indicator of a Society's Quality of Life

    c. Childhood Mortality Rate (CMR): Annual Number of Children Between 1 and 5 Years Old Who Die per 1,000 Births

    d. Factors that Contribute to High IMR and CMR Include Diarrhea (Often Caused by Disease-Infested Water), Improper Weaning, Famine, Malnutrition, Poor Health of the Mother, and Inadequate Prenatal Care

B. What Is the Relationship Between Women's Status and Population Growth?

1. If Women's Status is Low:

    a. Motherhood Only Option

    b. Birth Rates Rise

2. Status Determined By:

    a. Access to Education

    b. Access to Adequate Health Care

    c. Legal Rights

    d Employment Opportunities Outside Home

e. Wage Earnings

f. Marriage Age

g. Number of Children

Learning Objectives

After learning the material in Chapter 8 you should be able to:

1. Explain the basic arguments of each side in the Great Population Debate.

2. Explain how the human population can be considered a resource.

3. Define demography and discuss the demographic statistics pertaining to population size and growth (how populations are measured and what information those statistics reveal).

4. Discuss the different factors affecting population growth rates.

5. Describe the relationship between carrying capacity and population growth.

6. Discuss how demographic statistics are indicators of the quality of life for a particular nation.

7. Compare population growth and quality of life in the more-developed countries and the less-developed countries.

Did You Know . . . ?

240 children are born throughout the world every minute.

Key Concepts

Read this summary of Chapter 8 and identify the important concepts discussed in the chapter.

Whether or not one defines human population growth as a problem is at the heart of the great population debate. On one side of the debate are, among others, Cornucopians, who believe that human population growth presents no problem and indeed, that continued growth is desirable because more people means more consumers, more ideas, more human inventiveness. On the other side of the debate are Malthusians, proponents of the beliefs credited to Thomas Malthus, an eighteenth-century parson who believed that humans tend to reproduce out of an innate desire to procreate. According to Malthus, that tendency is offset by food production, which is limited; war, famine, and pestilence act as negative feedbacks that help to limit population growth. Moreover, the poor are disproportionately affected since they cannot afford to buy food supplies or medicines, and are more likely to be sent off to war. Neomalthusians agree that there is a link between poverty and family size, but argue that food may not be as important a factor as Malthus believed.

The scientific study of the sum of individual population acts is called demography. Demographers study how populations change over time in order to understand the causes and consequences of human population dynamics. Populations are typically measured in one of two ways: absolute number of people or growth rate. The actual increase (or decrease) in absolute numbers is given as (the number of births + immigration) - (the number of deaths + emigration). The growth rate is defined as the difference between the crude birth rate (number of live births per 1,000 people) and the crude death rate (number of deaths per 1,000 people), expressed as a percentage. When births are equal to deaths, the growth rate is zero, and the condition is known as zero population growth (ZPG).

Most of the people born in the coming decades will live in less-developed countries (LDCs). LDCs all have the fastest doubling times, the number of years it will take a population to double, assuming that the current growth rate remains constant.

Growth rates are affected by migration, fertility, and the population's age distribution. When births are equal to deaths, and migration is equal to immigration, the growth rate is zero. Measures of fertility, the actual bearing of offspring, include the general fertility rate, the age-specific fertility rate, and the total fertility rate. Population momentum occurs when there are large numbers of children living as fertility rates begin to drop; the population, in terms of absolute numbers, continues to grow significantly because there are more people entering their childbearing years. The age distribution of a population is graphically represented by a population profile, an age structure histogram that employs horizontal bars to depict the number of males and females of each age group.

Population profiles for LDCs typically have a pyramidal shape because the largest group within the population is the young (under 15) and the smallest is the elderly (over 65). The age distribution of a population reveals important information about the population's future growth (if there are many young people, the population will continue to experience population momentum) and dependency load (a significant proportion of young or old means a higher dependency load for those who are working). Population growth also affects both GNP and per capita GNP; high growth or a large proportion of elderly places a greater strain on a government to provide basic services (roads, schools, hospitals, etc.).

Calculating the carrying capacity of environments for human populations requires factoring in the quality of life a population aspires to. Determining cultural carrying capacity is difficult and imprecise but necessary if we are to achieve a balance between the human population and the ability of the environment to sustain life. Four demographic factors reveal significant information about the quality of life of the majority of people in a given society: population density, how closely people are grouped; urbanization, a rise in the number and size of cities; life expectancy at birth, the average number of years a newborn can be expected to live; and infant and childhood mortality, the number of infants under age 1 who die each year per 1,000 live births and the number of children between the ages of 1 and 5 who die each year per 1,000 live births, respectively. The infant mortality rate is widely considered the single best indicator of a society's quality of life. IMRs, whether in LDCs or among the poor in MDCs, could be lowered if all people had access to clean water, sanitation, and adequate health care, and if mothers are given the education and health services needed to care for their children.

Improving women's status could help to lower population growth by opening new avenues to them beyond motherhood. Women's status is reflected in access to education, access to adequate health care, legal rights, employment opportunities outside the home, wage earnings, marriage age, and number of children.

Key Terms

age-specific fertility rate

childhood mortality rate

crude birth rate (CBR)

crude death rate (CDR)

cultural carrying capacity

demography

dependency load

doubling time

emigration

environmental refugee

fertility

general fertility rate

growth rate

immigration

infant mortality rate

life expectancy

migration

population momentum

population profile

replacement fertility

total fertility rate (TFR)

urbanization

vital statistics

zero population growth (ZPG)

Environmental Success Story

In 1985, after county officials announced plans to build a $36 million incinerator near their Canton, New York home, Paul and Ellen Connett started their war against mass burning of waste. As more than 200 government jurisdictions look at the idea of incineration as a means of dealing with overflowing landfills, Paul has talked more than 400 times in 36 states about the importance of recycling, composting, and not creating waste in the first place. Ellen produces a weekly newsletter called "Waste Not" that keeps citizens up to date on the issues of incineration. Even with all of the information about the dangers of incineration, the Connetts say the major problem in the battle is the close-mindedness of people.

True/False

1. Of the more than 5 billion people in the world, over 4 billion   T   F
   live in LDCs.

2. Migration into a country or region is called emigration.   T   F

3. Africa, western and southern Asia, and Central America are   T   F
   the regions with the highest growth rates.

4. The carrying capacity for human populations is determined   T   F
   in the same way as non-human populations.

5. The infant mortality rate in the U.S. is much lower than that   T   F
   of other industrialized nations.

Fill in the Blank

1. The number of live births per 1,000 people is a statistic called the _____ .

2. The fertility rate needed to ensure that each set of parents is replaced by their
   offspring is known as the _____ .

3. _____ occurs when there are large numbers of children
   living as fertility rates begin to drop.

4. In order for a nation's economy to grow, for every 1% increase in population
   growth, the _____ should increase by 3%.

5. The _____ rate is the most significant factor that keeps the
   average life expectancy for the developing world below that of the developed
   world.

Multiple Choice

Choose the best answer.

1. The world's three most populous countries are
   A. China, the former U.S.S.R., and Bangladesh.
   B. China, India, and the former U.S.S.R.
   C. China, India, and the U.S.
   D. China, India, and Bangladesh.

2. If the crude birth rate is 32/1,000 and the crude death rate is 12/1,000, what is the growth rate?
   A. 4.4%
   B. 2.7%
   C. 2.0%
   D. 0.2%

3. World population is expected to stabilize at around _____ at the start of the 22nd century.
   A. 22.5 billion
   B. 20 billion
   C. 12 billion
   D. 5.4 billion

4. The doubling time for a country whose population is growing at 1.4% would be
   A. 50 years.
   B. 20 years.
   C. 9.8 years.
   D. None of the above is true.

5. A country with zero population growth is
   A. Germany.
   B. Hungary.
   C. Italy.
   D. Denmark.

Short Answer

1. How is the actual population increase in absolute numbers determined for a particular country or region?

2. What is ZPG?

3. What is doubling time and how is it calculated?

4. List and briefly explain the three most important measures of fertility.

5. What demographic statistics are used to assess the quality of life?

Thought Questions

Develop a complete answer for each of the following.

1. How do cornucopians, Marxists, Malthusians, neomalthusians, and advocates of ZPG answer the question, "Is human population growth a problem?" Explain the reasoning behind each of their answers.

2. Explain why "third world" is a value-laden term. How does this label reflect values placed on different human populations? What might be the effects of such labels?

3. What is the growth rate, and how is it determined? How do demographers use the growth rate, and why is it sometimes misleading?

4. Discuss the factors that contribute to the rapid population growth in LDCs.

5. Contrast the population profile of a developing country with that of a developed country. What social and economic implications do the differences have?

6. What is the relationship between population growth and economic development? Use examples from Ethiopia to illustrate.

7. What are the factors which distinguish human carrying capacity from non-human carrying capacity? Explain the concept of cultural carrying capacity.

8. Discuss the causes and effects of urbanization.

Related Concepts

Describe the relationship. (There may be more than one.)

BETWEEN...	AND...
natural growth rate	actual growth rate
total fertility rate in MDCs	total fertility rate in LDCs
status of women	population growth
standard of living	resource use
carrying capacity	cultural carrying capacity

Suggested Activities

1. Write a letter to the editor of your local newspaper arguing for your position in the Great Population Debate.

2. What will life be like in the U.S. in 2025, when world population reaches 10 billion? Alternatively, what will life be like in Bangladesh or Mexico City? Describe in writing what you imagine.

3. Read *The Ultimate Resource* by Julian Simon.

4. Read *The Population Explosion* by Drs. Paul and Anne Ehrlich.

CHAPTER 9

Managing Human Population Growth

Chapter Outline

I. History of Management of Human Population Growth: How Has the Human Population Grown Historically?

   A. Early Hunter-Gatherers

      1. Nomadic, With a Strong Sense of the Earth

      2. Practiced Intentional Birth Control

   B. Rise of Agriculture

      1. Necessary for Survival

         a. Animals Became Extinct Via Predation and Altered Habitats

         b. Humans Begin to Cultivate Own Food

      2. Agriculture as Impetus for Having Children for Labor Source

   C. Rise of Agriculture Gives Rise to Cities

      1. Food Produced In Country Consumed In City

         a. Food Wastes No Longer Returned to Soil

         b. Soil Becomes Less Productive

      2. Cities Concentrate the Waste of Populations

      3. Population Control in Medieval Societies

         a. Infanticide

         b. Plagues

D. Industrialization

    1. View of Children During Early Phases of Industrial Growth

        a. Valued as Cheap Source of Income and Cheap Labor

        b. Exponential Growth of Populations

    2. By 1900s, Birth Rate in Industrialized World Drops

        a. Rise in Standards of Living

        b. Safe and Inexpensive Means of Birth Control Introduced

        c. Increase in the Cost of Child Rearing

II. What Are the Demographic Transition and the Demographic Trap?

A. Demographic Transition

    1. Population Path Followed by Industrialized Nations

    2. Transition as a Result of Four Stages

        a. Stage One: Birth/Death Rates Both High

        b. Stage Two: Death Rates Fall; Birth Rates Remain High; Growth Rate Rises

        c. Stage Three: Birth Rates Fall as Standard of Living Rises; Growth Rate Falls

        d. Stage Four: Growth Rate Continues to Fall to Zero or to a Negative Rate

B. Demographic Trap

    1. Population Path of Most Developing Nations

    2. Caught or "Trapped" in Stage Two of Demographic Transition

        a. Before 1970, LDCs Seemed Poised to Make Transition Thanks to Economic Growth

        b. Since 1970, Economic Growth has not Kept Pace with Population

      c. High Birth/Low Death Rates; Explosive Population Growth

      d. Downward Spiral in Standard of Living

III. What Policies Are Used to Control Population Growth?

  A. Population Policies

    1. Planned Course of Action or Inaction Taken By a Government

    2. Designed to Influence Choices or Decisions on Fertility/Migration

  B. United States Government with Unofficial Pronatalist Position

    1. Income Tax Deductions for All Children

    2. Movement to Limit Legal Abortions

    3. Increased Benefits for Each Child Born into a Welfare Family

    4. Belief that Economy Based on Continued Population Growth

    5. Belief that Family Size Should Be Decided by the Family

  C. People's Republic of China with Antinatalist Policy

    1. Implemented Laws on a Marrying Age for Women

    2. Payments to Couples Who Delay Having Children

    3. Tax Structure that Penalizes Large Families

IV. What Are the Arguments in Favor of Controlling Population Growth?

  A. Arguments Opposing Any Growth in Population

    1. Ultimately Leads to Environmental Degradation

    2. Results in Worsened Living Conditions

    3. Lowers the Carrying Capacity

    4. Belief that Violent Conflict and Population Growth Are Interrelated

  B. Arguments Opposing Only Rapid Population Growth (Not Growth In

General)

    1. Negatively Impacts Economic Development

    2. Negatively Impacts Living Standards

    3. Negatively Impacts Programs that Improve People's Lives

V. What Is Family Planning?

    A. Measures Enabling Parents to Control Number of Children and Spacing of Births

    B. Goals of Family Planning:

        1. For Couples To Have Healthy Children

        2. For Couples To Care for Their Children

        3. For Couples To Have the Number of Children that They Want

        4. May or May Not Limit Number of Children

    C. China's Program

        1. Nation with Best Known Population Control Program

        2. Reasons Chinese Government Initiated Population Control Measures

            a. Freshwater and Food at a Premium for Nation's Population

            b. Country Experiencing Population Momentum

        3. Government Perks/Coercive Measures for Citizen Compliance

            a. Free Education and Health Care

            b. Increased Personal and Family Incomes

            c. Increased Legal Marrying Age for Women

            d. Contraceptives, Abortions, Sterilizations Free of Charge

            e. Preferential Housing, Retirement Income Granted for Conformity

VI. What Methods Are Used to Control Births?

    A. Preconception Birth Control Methods

        1. Barrier Methods

            a. Condom

            b. Vaginal Sponge

            c. Diaphragm

            d. Spermicides

        2. Hormonal Contraceptives

            a. Pill

            b. Injections and Implants

        3. Sterilization

    B. Postconception Birth Control Methods

        1. Intrauterine Device

        2. RU-486 Pill

        3. Abortion

    C. Contraceptive Use Worldwide

VII. Future Management of Human Population Growth

    A. Protect Human Health and the Environment

    B. Prevent Resource Abuse through Conservation

    C. Preserve Living Systems

Learning Objectives

After learning the material in Chapter 9 you should be able to:

1. Briefly recount how the human population has grown historically.

2. Describe the demographic transition, identify the factors needed for the transition to occur, and explain what is meant by the demographic trap.

3. Define population policy and explain how policies can be used to encourage or discourage growth.

4. Discuss the goals and components of China's population control program.

5. Summarize the arguments given in favor of controlling or limiting population growth.

6. Discuss the difference between family planning and birth control; give examples of each.

Did You Know . . . ?

Africa has the highest birth rate in the world.

Key Concepts

Read this summary of Chapter 9 and identify the important concepts discussed in the chapter.

For most of its tenure on Earth, beginning some 40,000 or 50,000 years ago, *Homo sapiens* existed by gathering wild plants and hunting wild animals. Tribal groups controlled their populations through abstinence from sexual intercourse, birth spacing, and infanticide. Some 10,000 to 12,000 years ago, the last ice age came to an end and the climate began to warm significantly. Human predation and loss of habitat (caused by the warming) led to the extinction of numerous species of large mammals. Human tribes were forced to begin to cultivate more of their foods, and some abandoned their nomadic lifestyle for a more settled lifestyle. Children became valued because they could help with household and agricultural chores. Consequently, with the rise of agriculture populations began to grow more rapidly and the environmental impact of human activities increased. Advances in death control ushered in a period of rapid growth. Birth rates in the western world began to fall with the onset of the Industrial Revolution and subsequent rising standard of living, the introduction of safe and reliable means of birth control, and an increase in the cost of child rearing.

However, the population continued to grow (though more slowly) because there were so many more people in total.

The population path followed by the industrialized nations, the demographic transition, describes the movement of a nation from high growth to low growth. There are four stages in the demographic transition. In stage 1, birth and death rates are both high; birth rates are actually fairly constant but death rates fluctuate as seasonal and cyclic factors (disease, harsh or mild weather, etc.) come into play. In stage 2, death rates fall but birth rates remain high and the population undergoes rapid growth. In stage 3, economic development improves the society's standard of living and birth rates begin to fall; the growth rate also begins to fall and nears zero. Eventually, the population's growth rate declines to a zero or negative rate, an indicator of a population in stage 4 of the demographic transition.

Nations in the developing world have found it difficult, if not impossible, to follow the path of demographic transition. Much of the growth in the global population in the past fifty years has occurred in LDCs; falling death rates and constant or slightly rising birth and fertility rates are responsible for this growth. Economic development has failed to keep pace with population growth; rapid growth and the environmental deterioration it causes are causing a downward spiral in the standard of living. Some developing nations are thus caught in a demographic trap, unable to break out of stage 2 of the demographic transition.

Any planned course of action taken by a government designed to influence its constituents' choices or decisions on fertility or migration can be considered a population policy. A pronatalist policy encourages natality or births; an antinatalist policy discourages births. Pronatalist or antinatalist policies are developed as a result of the way population changes are perceived.

Family planning is an umbrella term used to describe a wide variety of measures that enable parents to control the number of children they have and the spacing of their children's births. Its goal is not to limit births, though it may be used to do so; rather, the goal of family planning is to enable couples to have healthy children, to care for their children, and to have the number of children they want. China became the first nation to have as an official goal the end of population growth and the subsequent lowering of absolute numbers by a significant amount. From 1969 to 1979 China achieved a transition from high to low birth rates by implementing the strongest family planning measures ever attempted.

Birth control can be achieved through various preconception and postconception methods. Natural forms of contraception, such as rhythm, have a high failure rate. Rhythm can be fairly effective but its effectiveness depends on a fairly sophisticated knowledge of body processes and on cooperation between spouses. Other forms of preconception birth control methods include barrier methods (condoms, spermicides, vaginal sponge, and the diaphragm), hormonal

97

contraceptives (the pill, injections, or implants), and sterilization. Postconception birth control methods include the intrauterine device, the RU-486 pill, and abortion. The abortion controversy revolves around the conflict between religious and moral beliefs about the status of the fetus.

Worldwide, contraceptive use varies widely. People in the industrial nations enjoy easy access to birth control methods, while those in the developing nations, in general, do not. Contraceptive use also varies widely within the United States.

Key Terms

abortion

antinatalist policy

demographic transition

demographic trap

family planning

population policy

pronatalist policy

Environmental Success Story

Mechai Viravaida, who founded the Population and Community Development Association in 1974, has been the driving force in trying to cut population growth in Thailand. He has used many ingenious methods to get his message out: using brightly colored condoms as business cards, handing out condoms in traffic jams, and even paying car insurance for taxi drivers who sell a quota of condoms, just to name a few. He has set up thousands of family planning centers that the government encourages. The dominant religion in Thailand does not carry a taboo against family planning; this has assisted in reducing the population growth rate from 3.2% in 1970 to 1.7% in 1988.

True/False

1. The basic goal of family planning is to limit births.   T   F

2. Advances in death control, rather than increased birth rates, T F
   led to rapid population growth during the Industrial
   Revolution.

3. In general, the nations with the highest average per capita T F
   incomes have rates of population growth that are
   considerably above the world average.

4. Compared to less educated women, better educated women T F
   are more likely to have large families.

5. The only 100 percent effective method of birth control is T F
   abstention.

Fill in the Blank

1. The _____ is the movement of the population of a
   nation from high growth to low growth.

2. Any planned course of action or inaction taken by a government designed to
   influence its constituents' choices or decisions on fertility or migration can be
   considered a _____ .

3. _____ includes a wide variety of measures that enable
   parents to control the number of children they have and the spacing of their
   children's births.

4. Spermicides, hormonal contraceptives, and sterilization are examples of
   _____ birth control methods.

5. Nations that are unable to break out of the second stage of the demographic
   transition are said to be in a _____.

Multiple Choice

Choose the best answer.

1. When people first began to practice agriculture about 10,000 years ago, the population of the earth was probably about
   A. 1 million.
   B. 2 million.
   C. 5 million.
   D. 10 million.

2. The three most popular methods of birth control worldwide are
   A. the pill, IUDs, and rhythm method.
   B. the pill, sterilization, and the condom.
   C. sterilization, IUDs, and the pill.
   D. sterilization, the pill, and condoms.

3. The Chinese government estimates China's carrying capacity at about _ _ people.
   A. 5 billion
   B. 2 billion
   C. 700 million
   D. 500 million

4. Excluding abstention, the most effective method of preconception birth control is
   A. the pill.
   B. condom with spermicide.
   C. diaphragm.
   D. IUD.

5. All of the following are postconception birth control methods except
   A. Depo-Provera.
   B. abortion.
   C. IUD.
   D. RU-486 pill.

Short Answer

1. What is the Mexico City policy?

2. What is family planning?

3. In the U.S., which two groups are least likely to use birth control?

4. What three factors contributed to lower population growth in the industrialized world around 1900?

5. What are the four stages of the demographic transition?

Thought Questions

Develop a complete answer for each of the following.

1. Discuss the growth of human population throughout history, beginning with early hunter-gatherers and moving through the onset of agriculture, the rise of cities, and the Industrial Revolution.

2. Describe the four phases of the demographic transition. Also explain the demographic trap being experienced by some developing countries.

3. Define population policy. What are indications that the U.S. has an unofficial pronatalist policy? Give examples of pronatalist and antinatalist policies from other countries.

4. Outline the arguments in favor of controlling or limiting population growth.

5. Explain how contraceptive use differs between LDCs and MDCs. Which are most effective in LDCs? in MDCs? Discuss the reasons for these differences.

Did You Know . . . ?

To accommodate the growing population, nearly 3,500 acres of rural land are bulldozed in the United States each day to create space for new buildings, highways, and other development.

Suggested Activities

1. Think about your own views and those of your family or community. Do you believe population growth should be controlled? What values do you have that determine your answer to this question?

CHAPTER 10

Food Resources, Hunger, and Poverty

Chapter Outline

I. Describing Food Resources: Biological Boundaries

   A. What Are the Components of a Healthy Diet?

      1. The Body Needs Food for Three Main Reasons:

         a. To Supply the Energy Needed to Do Work

         b. To Grow and Develop

         c. Regulate Life Processes

      2. Essential Elements for Life:

         a. Macronutrients -- Required By the Body in Large Amounts

            1. Carbohydrates and Fats (Primary Energy Source to Do Work)

            2. Proteins (the Body's "Building Blocks")

         b. Micronutrients -- Required by the Body in Trace Amounts

            1. Iron

            2. Vitamins

   B. What Is the Current Status of Food Production?

      1. Foods the Global Population Relies On:

         a. Staples -- Important Foods in Many People's Lives

         b. Top Four Food Crops Worldwide:

            1. Wheat

            2. Rice

3. Maize

4. Potatoes

2. Food Security

   a. Defined As the Ability of a Nation to Feed Itself on an On-going Basis

   b. Gains that Have Been Made in Food Production Per Acre Offset By:

      1. Population Growth

      2. Social Inequities

      3. Increase in Degraded Cropland; Cropland Converted to Nonfarm Use

II. Physical Boundaries: Where Does Our Food Come From?

   A. Available Fertile Land

      1. About 11% of Earth's Land Can Easily Produce Food

      2. Intense Management

   B. Aquatic Harvest

      1. 11% of Land Surface Can Be Used to Produce Food

      2. Earth's Fertility is not Evenly Distributed

      3. Proper Management Should Enable Food to Meet Needs for Humans

III. Social Boundaries

   A. What Is Hunger and How Does It Affect Human Health?

      1. Starvation and Famine

         a. Starvation Is Defined As Suffering/Death from Deprivation of Nourishment

         b. Famine is Widespread Starvation as a Result of Many Factors

            1. Catastrophic Natural Events

2. Human Activity, Such as War, Inequitable Land Distribution

2. Undernutrition and Malnutrition

   a. Chronic Undernutrition

      1. Defined as the Consumption of Too Few Calories/Protein Over Extended Period of Time

      2. Regular Consumption of Fewer than 2,000 Calories

   b. Malnutrition

      1. Generally Defined as the Consumption of Too Little of the Specific Nutrients Essential for Good Health

      2. Able to Maim and Deform

   c. Malabsorptive Hunger

      1. Often Accompanies Undernutrition and Malnourishment

      2. Body Loses Ability to Absorb Nutrients from Food Consumed

      3. Caused by Parasites in Digestive Tract; Severe Protein Deficiency

3. Nutritional Diseases

   a. Kwashiorkor

      1. Correct Calorie Count

      2. Insufficient Protein Intake

   b. Marasmus

      1. Deficient Calorie Count

      2. Deficient Protein Intake

4. Seasonal Hunger

   a. Way of Life, Part of Annual Cycle for Many

   b. Occurs at a Time Before the New Harvest When Old Harvest Runs Out

   c. United States Version -- End of Month When Food Stamps Run Out

B. Who Are the Hungry?

1. Where Hunger Occurs

    a. Usually Thought to Occur in Third World Nations

    b. Hunger and Dietary Diseases Also Prevalent in U.S.

2. Relationship Between Hunger and Poverty

    a. Hungry All Share Common Characteristic of Being Poor

    b. How Poor is Poor?

        1. Compare Income with the Price of Buying Food Items

        2. Physical Quality of Life Index

3. Relationship Between Poverty and Environmental Degradation

    a. Hungry Forced to Degrade Environment to Support Self

    b. Degraded Environment Offers Little to Support Environment, with more Poverty As a Result

4. Why Hunger Exists in a World of Plenty

    a. Natural Environmental Conditions Account for Inequities

        1. Some Areas More Fertile, Better Growing Conditions

        2. Some Areas Less Productive, More Vulnerable to Injury

    b. Hunger Exists Due to Lack of Political Will to Fight It

    c. Various Economic Factors Create/Exacerbate Poverty

        1. Best Lands Controlled by Small Numbers of Wealthy Landowners

        2. Existence of Cash Crops for Export

IV. History of Management of Food Resources

  A. How Have Humans Manipulated Food Resources in the Past

    1. Domestication

        a. Result of Selection of Traits Useful for Survival in Captivity

        b. Plant and Animal Domestication Led to Rise of Agriculture

105

2. Agriculture

    a. Purposeful Tending of a Particular Plant/Animal Species for Human Use

    b. Land Races -- Varieties of Plants Adapted for Local Conditions

B. Changes in Food Production

    1. Changes in the Developed World

        a. Agriculture Now Fossil Fuel Intensive

            1. Fertilizers and Pesticides Petroleum-based Products

            2. Large Machinery Dependent Upon Fossil Fuels

        b. Farming as an Agribusiness

            1. Traditional Farms Purchased by Large Corporations

            2. Agriculture -- Way of Life

            3. Agribusiness -- Economic Venture

    2. Changes in the Developing World

        a. Green Revolution -- High-yield Plant Varieties Enable the Doubling of Crop Production

        b. High-yield Plants Vulnerable to Dise

C. Importance of Genetic Diversity

    1. The Gene Bank

        a. Place Where Germplasm of Plant Species is Preserved for Future Use

        b. In Vitro Preservation

            1. Plant Tissue Stored in Test Tube

            2. Allows Storage of Many Species for Up to Two Years

            3. Drawbacks Include Temporary Storage

        c. Cryopreservation

            1. Storing Plant and Animal Materials in Liquid Nitrogen

2. May Prove to Longer and Safer Storage Form

   2. Issue of Access to Gene Banks

     a. Patented Breeds of Crop Species Expensive

     b. Exploitive to LDCs, Whose Native Plants Are Often the Source of High-yield Varieties

D. Increasing Food Production

   1. Aquaculture -- Production of Aquatic Plants/Animals in Controlled Environment

   2. Biotechnology -- Organisms or Their Parts used to Manufacture Food Products

V. Future Management of Food Resources

A. Prevent Resource Abuse Through Conservation

B. Protect Human Health and the Environment

C. Preserve Living Systems

Learning Objectives

After learning the material in Chapter 10 you should be able to:

1. Identify the critical components of a healthy diet.

2. Identify the major foods relied upon by the global human population and summarize the current status of food production.

3. Describe the various manifestations of hunger and explain how hunger affects human health.

4. Discuss how food consumption patterns vary worldwide.

5. Describe the relationship among hunger, poverty, and environmental degradation.

6. List various reasons why hunger continues to be a problem.

7. Briefly describe how food production patterns have changed in the past fifty years in both the developed and the developing worlds, and identify problems with modern agriculture in both MDCs and LDCs.

8. Explain the role of gene banks, biotechnology, and aquaculture in food production.

Did You Know ... ?

Worldwide, 27 children die of starvation every minute.

Key Concepts

Read this summary of Chapter 10 and identify the important concepts discussed in the chapter.

Carbohydrates and fats are the major sources of the energy required to maintain the body and perform work. Proteins are the "building blocks" of the body, forming the substance of muscles, organs, antibodies, and enzymes.

Of the 80,000 potentially edible crops on earth, global agriculture is dependent on only a few plant species. Just eight crops supply 75% of the human diet, with the top four being wheat, rice, corn (maize), and potatoes. Agriculture also relies on just a small number of animals. Meat production can cause problems when it is practiced to the extent and in the manner common in the developed world. When livestock are fed grains, the efficiency of food production is greatly reduced.

Food security is the ability of a nation to feed itself on an ongoing basis. Building our reserve supply of grain is a task which is becoming increasingly more difficult.

Most of the world's hungry live in LDCs. The most extreme and dramatic effect of hunger is starvation, suffering or death from the deprivation of nourishment. Widespread starvation, or famine, such as that which occurred in Somalia in 1992, is the result of many interrelated factors, including war, prolonged drought, production of cash crops, unequal distribution systems, and unequal distribution of lands. Each year, however, of the deaths attributed to hunger, most come not from starvation but from undernutrition, the consumption of too few calories and proteins over an extended period of time; malnutrition, consumption of too little (or infrequently, too much) of specific nutrients essential for good health;

malabsorptive hunger, the body's loss of the ability to absorb nutrients from the food consumed; and hunger-related diseases, such as kwashiorkor and marasmus.

Worldwide, about one in five people suffers from chronic hunger. About 40 percent of the world's hungry are children; most of the rest are women. Most of the world's hungry live in the developing world within the "great hunger belt," a region encompassing various nations in Southeast Asia, the Indian subcontinent, the Middle East, Africa, and the equatorial region of Latin America. Five nations -- India, Bangladesh, Nigeria, Pakistan, and Indonesia -- together house one-half of the world's hungry. It is important to remember, however, that even within the wealthiest industrial nations, some people go hungry. No matter where they live, the hungry share a common characteristic: poverty.

There is a very real connection between hunger, poverty, and environmental degradation. Although much of the world's environmental degradation is due to affluence in MDCs, poverty, especially in LDCs, also causes environmental degradation. The poor are forced to cultivate marginal lands, overgraze grasslands and pastures, or clear forests. Hunger and poverty trap the poor in a vicious cycle. Given less food and nutrients, the poor are less able to work and learn and more prone to disease; lack of education or poor work performance prolongs or exacerbates poverty, as does chronic illness. For many, death is the only way out of the cycle of hunger and poverty.

Food production, especially of grains, is sufficient to feed the world's people, yet hunger persists in our world. Its causes are many: Natural environmental conditions which account for disparities in food production; economic and political institutions which concentrate power so that some people are left with none; inequalities in land ownership; and cash crop production.

In the past fifty years food production in the United States has come to rely heavily on inputs of energy, water, synthetic fertilizers, herbicides and pesticides. Traditional agriculture has given way to agribusiness. In the developing world, the green revolution, sparked by the use of high-yield varieties of crops, promised to make nations self-sufficient in food production. But despite its successes worldwide, the green revolution has not ended hunger in the developing world. In recent years the international community has begun several efforts to protect genetic diversity (through gene banking) and increase world food production (through the addition of new plants to the human diet, aquaculture, biotechnology).

Key Terms

agribusiness

agriculture

amino acids

aquaculture

biotechnology

chronic undernutrition

cryopreservation

domestication

famine

food security

gene bank

genetic engineering

green revolution

kwashiorkor

land race

malabsorptive hunger

malnutrition

marasmus

monoculture

polyculture

seasonal hunger

staple

starvation

tissue culture

Environmental Success Story

Perkasie, a tiny town of 6,900, 25 miles south of Philadelphia, has come up with a new way to get its residents to recycle their trash. The method has been to charge $1.50 for each 40-pound garbage bag that a family sets out on the curb. When the town began its program, it reduced its disposal of garbage by half. Instead of picking up garbage twice a week, one day was used for collecting recyclables. The per-bag fee, combined with the threat of a fine, has lowered the town's cost of garbage collection by 30 percent and the cost of garbage disposal by nearly 40 percent. In today's wasteful society, Perkasie should be considered a town to follow, considering its participation is nearly 90 percent.

True/False

1. The nine essential amino acids are those that are synthesized   T   F
   by the body.

2. More land is used for grazing livestock than for growing   T   F
   crops.

3. On average, people in MDCs consume about 10% more   T   F
   calories than necessary.

4. About one in every five people in the world suffers from   T   F
   chronic hunger.

5. Aquaculture is the fastest growing sector of agriculture in the   T   F
   U.S.

Fill in the Blank

1. _____ and_____ are the major sources of energy for
   the body.

2. About 10% of the world's protein supply comes from _____.

3. _____ is a type of hunger that can be caused by parasites in the intestinal tract.

4. Varieties of plants that are adapted to local conditions are called _____ .

5. The process of storing plant or animal tissue in liquid nitrogen is called

_____ .

Multiple Choice

Choose the best answer.

1. Complex carbohydrates, protein, and fat are examples of
   A. micronutrients.
   B. macronutrients.
   C. staples.
   D. None of the above is true.

2. At most, the percent of ice-free land which could be used to grow crops is about
   A. 11%.
   B. 22%.
   C. 33%.
   D. None of the above is true..

3. Worldwide, the number of infants and young children who die each year from hunger and hunger-related diseases is estimated to be around
   A. 5 million.
   B. 15 million.
   C. 25 million.
   D. 40 million.

4. A diseased caused by a lack of protein and too few calories is
   A. marasmus.
   B. kwashiorkor.
   C. malabsorptive hunger.
   D. amaranth.

5. The number of potentially edible crops on earth is estimated to be
   A. 25,000.
   B. 50,000.
   C. 80,000.
   D. None of the above is true.

Short Answer

1. Why are proteins important for a healthy diet?

2. What are the top four food crops in the world?

3. What is famine?

4. What is the "great hunger belt?"

5. What three factors determine the PQLI?

Thought Questions

Develop a complete answer for each of the following.

1. Describe a healthy diet.

2. What kinds of hunger are there? Explain the situations that lead to each.

3. Explain the energy investment required to support a diet with a high meat content. Discuss the fact that people in MDCs consume twice as much meat as people in LDCs.

4. Where does hunger occur? Compare the diets of people in MDCs and LDCs, wealthy people and poor people.

5. Why does hunger exist?

6. Compare pre-1950 agriculture in the developed world with agriculture today. Explain why, even though grain production per hectare has increased, there are more hungry people than there were ten years ago. How have HYV's and cash crops contributed to the situation?

7. Describe the various techniques being used to preserve genetic diversity of crop plants. Why is this work important?

Related Concepts

Describe the relationship. (There may be more than one.)

BETWEEN...	AND...
malnutrition	undernutrition
hunger in LDCs	hunger in MDCs
Physical Quality of Life Index	poverty
poverty	environmental degradation
democracy	hunger

Did You Know . . . ?

The food term "natural" has no legal meaning and may be used on almost any food.

Suggested Activities

1. Keep a "food diary" of everything you eat each day for one week. How many calories do you consume? What percentage of calories come from fat, protein, and carbohydrates?

2. Find out more about hunger in your area. Who are the hungry? Why do they remain hungry in a world of plenty?

3. Try an experiment: for two weeks, modify your diet to include more foods that are produced locally.

CHAPTER 11

Energy Issues

Chapter Outline

I. Describing Energy Resources

    A. Physical Boundaries

        1. What Is Energy and How Is It Measured?

        2. How Are Energy Resources Classified in Regard to Supply?

        3. What Is Energy Efficiency?

    B. Biological Boundaries

        1. What Is the Biological Significance of Energy Resources?

    C. Social Boundaries

        1. How Do Present Energy Consumption Patterns Vary Worldwide?

        2. What Important Environmental Issues Are Related to the Use of Energy Resources?

            a. Social Changes

            b. Environmental and Health Effects

            c. Dependence on Fossil Fuels

            d. Nuclear Power

            e. Energy Policy

Learning Objectives

After learning the material in Chapter 11 you should be able to:

1. Define energy and tell how it is measured.

2. Tell how energy resources are classified.

3. Define energy efficiency and summarize its environmental and economic benefits.

4. Describe how energy consumption patterns vary worldwide.

5. Describe the "Drain America First" policy and its association with national security.

6. Identify the problems associated with the use of fossil fuels and the use of nuclear power.

7. Discuss the energy policy controversy surrounding the Arctic National Wildlife Refuge.

Did You Know . . . ?

Between 1973 and 1988, energy use in the United States increased by 64 percent.

Key Concepts

Read this summary of Chapter 11 and identify the important concepts discussed in the chapter.

Energy, the capacity to do work, is measured in various units. Energy resources are generally classified as nonrenewable (exist in finite supply or are renewed at rates far slower than the rate of consumption), renewable (resupplied at rates faster than is consistent with use), or perpetual (inexhaustible).

In any energy conversion, although the same amount of energy exists before and after the conversion, not all of the energy remains useful. The conversion of energy from one form to another form always involves a change or degradation from a higher quality form to a lower quality form, and all forms of energy are ultimately degraded to heat energy. The efficiency of any system, device, or process that converts energy can be determined. Energy efficiency is a measure of the percentage of the total energy input that does useful work and is not converted to low temperature, low-quality heat. The net efficiency of a process or system that includes two or more energy conversions is found by determining the efficiency of each conversion. Efficiency is an important factor to bear in mind when purchasing an electrical appliance or gadget. The life-cycle cost of an item includes both the initial cost plus the operating costs, which will be lower for more efficient items.

Most of the world's energy is used by the developed countries; just 20 percent of the world's population uses 80 percent of the energy. Energy issues are complex and involve all aspects of our culture.

Environmental issues related to the use of energy can be grouped into five broad categories. These are social changes, environmental and health effects, dependence on fossil fuels, nuclear power, and energy policy. With respect to social changes, per capita consumption of energy in MDCs is currently 4 to 7 times higher than per capita consumption in LDCs, but LDCs are outpacing MDCs in terms of growth of energy consumption. As LDCs continue to try to develop economically, energy supplies will become more precious, and more threatened. Social changes are bound to occur.

As issue 2 suggests, all energy consumption affects the environment. The type and severity of these effects differ significantly according to the resource used. In general, renewable and perpetual resources are far more benign than fossil fuels.

With respect to issue 3, fossil fuels are the lifeblood of industrial societies, despite the problems they cause. However, our decades-long reliance on fossil fuels has greatly diminished supplies. Supplies of petroleum and natural gas are likely to be depleted by the middle of the next century.

Issue 4 pits proponents of nuclear power, who argue that it is a clean, safe, form of energy which can help reduce emissions of greenhouse gases, against those who argue that nuclear power is not inherently safe and that its drawbacks -- accidents, dismantling of old plants, and disposal of nuclear wastes -- are too severe to continue or increase our reliance on this resource.

The development of a coherent, long-range energy policy, issue 5, raises many important questions: What changes in life-styles, if any, will be necessary as supplies of petroleum continue to dwindle? What is the environmental cost of increasing our reliance on coal or nuclear power and how will those costs be offset? What conservation measures, if any, should be instituted to reduce our reliance on fossil fuels and ease the transition to alternative fuels? What measures should be taken, if any, to more quickly develop alternative energy resources?

Key Terms

alternative resource

conventional resource

energy

energy efficiency

life-cycle cost

net efficiency

nonrenewable resource

perpetual resource

renewable resource

Environmental Success Story

Since the oil embargo of the 1970s, Ellen Fletcher of Palo Alto, California has been on a crusade to establish rights for bicyclists. Her work has resulted in many improvements to the city: a two-mile stretch of road off limits to motorized vehicles, the requirement that new commercial and residential developments provide bicycle storage areas and new businesses provide showers for bike commuters, traffic lights adjusted so bicyclists have more time to cross intersections, a per-mile cash reimbursement for city workers who ride bicycles, and a program for juvenile traffic offenders which is conducted by the police department.

True/False

1. The sun is an example of a renewable resource.   T   F

2. Renewable and perpetual resources are called alternative   T   F
   resources.

3. Per capita energy consumption in MDCs is four to seven   T   F
   times greater than that in LDCs.

4. The construction of nuclear power plants has steadily   T   F
   increased in recent years.

5. The official energy policy of the U.S. government has been   T   F
   to "Drain America First."

Fill in the Blank

1. Fossil fuels are also called_____ because they are so commonly used.

2. _____ resources are supplied at rates faster than or consistent with use.

3. _____is a measure of the percentage of the total energy input that does useful work and is not converted into low temperature, low-quality heat.

4. The initial cost of an energy-efficient device plus the lifetime operating cost is called the _____.

5. The unofficial energy policy of the U.S. government has been to

_____ .

Multiple Choice

Choose the best answer.

1. Solar energy is an example of a
   A. nonrenewable resource.
   B. conventional resource.
   C. renewable resource.
   D. perpetual resource.

2. In the U.S., the percentage of energy supplied by renewable or perpetual sources is
A. 1%.
B. 4%.
C. 10%.
D. 14%.

3. Alternative energy sources provide about _____ of the world's energy.
A. 5%
B. 10%
C. 20%
D. 30%

4. Which of the following is true?
A. Per capita energy consumption in MDCs is greater than that in LDCs.
B. Energy consumption is growing faster in LDCs than in MDCs.
C. Energy consumption is increasing faster than the population in both MDCs and LDCs.
D. All of the above are true.

5. Approximately what percentage of U.S. electricity is provided by nuclear power?
A. 5%
B. 10%
C. 20%
D. 30%

Short Answer

1. Why do light bulbs get hot?

2. What is life-cycle cost?

3. What is energy efficiency?

4. What is an energy policy?

5. What is the first law of thermodynamics?

Thought Questions

Develop a complete answer for each of the following.

1. Explain the concept of net efficiency and discuss how it affects the economic and environmental costs of producing electricity.

2. Compare energy use in the developed world with energy use in the developing world.

3. Discuss the social changes that will be necessary if we are to conserve nonrenewable resources for uses other than supplying energy.

4. What are the implications of the industrialized world's dependence on fossil fuels?

5. Present the arguments for and against nuclear power.

6. What are the consequences for the U.S. of lacking an official energy policy? What are the arguments in favor of having one?

7. Using the Trans-Alaska Pipeline as an example, discuss how the areas of major energy issues presented in this chapter—social changes, environmental effects, dependence on fossil fuels, nuclear power, and energy policy are interconnected.

Related Concepts

Describe the relationship. (There may be more than one.)

BETWEEN...	AND...
perpetual resource	renewable resource
nonrenewable resource	conventional resource
energy conservation	economic development
energy policy	"drain America first"

Suggested Activities

1. Find out where the energy you use in your home comes from.

2. Organize a classroom debate on one or more of the energy issues presented in this chapter.

3. List the appliances in your home. If your energy supply were suddenly stopped, how would you manage without each appliance?

4. Try an experiment. Spend an entire day without using electricity or other types of energy. Share your experience with your classmates.

CHAPTER 12

Fossil Fuels

Environmental Humor--by Bart Kias

I have a solution to the shortage of natural gas: my uncle Al. If we ever run out, we can just pull his finger.

Chapter Outline

I. Describing Fossil Fuel Resources

    A. Biological Boundaries

        1. What Are Fossil Fuels?

        2. How Are Fossil Fuels Formed?

    B. Physical Boundaries

        1. Where Are Fossil Fuel Deposits Located?

    C. Social Boundaries

        1. What Is the Current Status of the World's Major Fossil Fuels?

            a. Coal

            b. Petroleum

            c. Natural Gas

            d. Minor Fossil Fuels: Oil Shales and Tar Sands

II. History of Management of Fossil Fuel Resources

    A. How Have Fossil Fuels Been Used Historically?

B. How Has Energy Consumption Changed in the United States?

C. What Was the 1973 OPEC Oil Embargo?

D. How Can We Increase Energy Efficiency?

   1. Industries

   2. Communities

   3. Individuals

III. Future Management of Fossil Fuel Resources

Learning Objectives

After learning the material in Chapter 12 you should be able to:

1. Identify the three major types of fossil fuels and explain briefly how fossil fuels were formed.

2. Differentiate between proven, subeconomic, and indicated reserves of fossil fuels.

3. Describe the current status (uses, availability, and environmental effects) of coal, petroleum, natural gas, oil shales, and tar sands.

4. Summarize how energy consumption has changed in the U.S. in the past 200 years.

5. Identify the Exxon *Valdez* accident and the problems that arose as a result.

6. Identify the 1973 OPEC Oil Embargo and its resulting consequences.

7. Give examples to illustrate how industries, communities, and individuals can increase energy efficiency and conserve fossil fuels.

Did You Know . . . ?

Three tons of gasoline are burned by the average car in its lifetime.

Key Concepts

Read this summary of Chapter 12 and identify the important concepts discussed in the chapter.

Coal, petroleum, and natural gas, the world's conventional fuels, are the fossilized remains of organic matter. Coal originated from plant matter, petroleum from aquatic organisms (algae and plankton), and oil from all types of organic matter, even cellulose. The processes that formed fossil fuels continue today, but because those processes are extremely slow, fossil fuels are classified as nonrenewable and finite. Fossil fuels are not distributed evenly beneath the earth's surface because the conditions that gave rise to the preservation and fossilization of organic matter did not occur everywhere.

The major fossil fuels are coal, petroleum, and natural gas. Minor fossil fuels are oil shales and tar sands. Coal, a solid composed primarily of carbon with small amounts of hydrogen, nitrogen, and sulfur, is the most abundant fossil fuel on earth. There are four types of coal. Anthracite coal has the highest carbon content and the lowest sulfur content; it is the most efficient and cleanest burning type of coal and the most preferred for heating homes and commercial buildings, but it is also the least abundant. Bituminous coal, the most common type, accounts for over half of U.S. reserves and has a heating value slightly lower than that of anthracite. It is preferred for electric power generation and the production of coke, which is used to make steel. Subbituminous and lignite coals, which together account for a little less than half of U.S. reserves, both have low heating values and must be burned in large amounts in order to heat effectively. However, these types contain very little sulfur, a desirable trait since sulfur emissions contribute to the formation of acid precipitation. Coal consumption declined over the past century but is expected to increase as reserves of petroleum dwindle and as reliance on nuclear power continues to slow. The majority of the world's coal reserves are located in the United States, the former Soviet Union, and China. U.S. reserves lie in three broad regions: Appalachian, central, and western or Rocky Mountain. Wyoming, Kentucky, and West Virginia are the three highest coal-producing states. Coal has the most serious environmental and health effects of all energy resources in use today. Problems include acid precipitation, acid mine drainage, air and water pollution, and carbon dioxide emissions, which exacerbate global climate change.

Petroleum, or crude oil, is a liquid composed primarily of hydrocarbon compounds. It is perhaps the most versatile of all fossil fuels, used to make products such as propane, gasoline, jet fuel, road tar, motor oil, and thousands of non-fuel substances and chemicals. The United States accounts for about 30 percent of the annual global consumption of petroleum (23 billion barrels). Gasoline is the most consumed petroleum product in the United States; the transportation sector accounts for about

60 percent of the nation's annual oil consumption. The greatest reserves of petroleum lie in the Middle East; other areas with sizable deposits include Latin America, the former Soviet Union, Africa, and North America. Like coal, petroleum has serious environmental consequences, including air pollution (its combustion releases carbon monoxide, sulfur oxides, nitrogen oxides, and hydrocarbons). Oil spills pose another serious threat to the environment.

Several different types of gas comprise natural gas; the most abundant is methane. Natural gas usually occurs along with petroleum and is known as associated gas. Increased attention has focused on natural gas because of our growing awareness of finite petroleum supplies and because gas is a much cleaner burning fuel than oil or coal. Compared to coal or petroleum, the combustion of natural gas releases far less carbon dioxide, nitrogen oxides, and sulfur oxides. Natural gas systems are also desirable because of their high conversion efficiency. Natural gas is a fairly abundant fuel; the world's largest deposits are in the former Soviet Union and the Middle East. In the United States, gas production is centered around the Gulf Coast, the midcontinent, and west Texas-east New Mexico.

Oil shales, fine-grained, compacted sedimentary rocks that contain varying amounts of a waxy, combustible organic matter called kerogen, and tar sands, sandstones that contain bitumen, a thick, high-sulfur, tarlike liquid, are minor fossil fuels. Extracting and refining these fuels are expensive and energy-intensive processes. Extraction also disturbs large areas of land, requires significant amounts of water, and produces a good deal of waste rock.

Humans have used fossil fuels for various purposes for thousands of years. Use as a fuel is relatively recent, at least for petroleum and natural gas. In the United States, wood was the leading fuel source for some two hundred years but was displaced by coal by 1885. In the early 1900s, coal met over 90 percent of the nation's energy needs. Coal's dominance ended with the widespread use of petroleum. By 1946, natural gas and petroleum together displaced coal as the chief energy source; by 1950, petroleum consumption alone outpaced coal consumption. In 1947, the United States became a net petroleum importer, a condition that persists today. The 1973 embargo by the Organization of Petroleum Exporting Countries curtailed supplies and the price of oil skyrocketed. An increased emphasis on conservation and energy efficiency resulted, but these were shortlived. Prices have since fallen, despite the occasional fear of shortages (such as that due to the Persian Gulf War), and conservation efforts have waned. But the world's supplies of fossil fuels are finite, and as supplies become increasingly scarce, their price will rise significantly. Increasingly, our reliance on fossil fuels will become economically and environmentally costly.

Key Terms

acid drainage

anthracite

associated gas

bituminous

coal

cogeneration

conservation revolution

economic reserve

fossil fuel

indicated reserve

inferred reserve

land subsidence

lignite

natural gas

nonassociated gas

oil shale

petroleum

proven reserve

subbituminous

subeconomic reserve

tar sand

Environmental Success Story

One day when Karen Blake of Buffalo, New York went out for a breath of fresh air, she came back into her house feeling very ill. She discovered that the problem was lawn care pesticides and fertilizers, and ever since, she has been fighting against them. She co-founded a group called Help Eliminate Lawn Pesticides (HELP), to warn others about the dangers of lawn chemicals. HELP brought the issue to the media, and in 1987 the state legislature passed a law that required chemical companies to have written contracts with customers, provide copies of warning labels of the chemicals being used, and post warning signs on yards for at least 24 hours after spraying. Even after this victory, Karen and HELP vow to fight lawn chemicals until they are banned.

True/False

1. Coal and petroleum originated largely from plant material.   T   F

2. Natural gas is the most abundant fossil fuel on earth.   T   F

3. Petroleum is primarily composed of a mixture of oxygen, sulfur, and nitrogen compounds.   T   F

4. Annual global usage of petroleum equals about 23 billion barrels.   T   F

5. Natural gas is the cleanest of all fossil fuels.   T   F

Fill in the Blank

1. The era in which most of the world's coal was formed was about _____ million years ago in the _____ period.

2. The energy contained in fossil fuels came originally from _____, captured by plants through _____ .

3. The petroleum deposits that have been located, measured, and inventoried are called _____.

4. The type of coal that burns most efficiently is _____ .

5. The simultaneous production of two useful forms of energy is called -_____ .

Multiple Choice

Choose the best answer.

1. Of what two elements are fossil fuels primarily made?
   A. carbon and oxygen
   B. hydrogen and oxygen
   C. carbon and hydrogen
   D. carbon and nitrogen

2. The most common type of coal in the U.S. is
   A. anthracite.
   B. bituminous.
   C. lignite.
   D. subbituminous.

3. U.S. coal reserves represent about_____of the nation's total energy resources.
   A. 50%
   B. 60%
   C. 80%
   D. 90%

4. The most productive coal-producing state is
   A. Montana.
   B. Kentucky.
   C. West Virginia.
   D. Wyoming.

5. Natural gas
   A. is primarily made up of methane, ethane, and propane.
   B. has about a 50% energy efficiency.
   C. is mostly used in the residential sector of the U.S.
   D. All of the above are true.

Short Answer

1. How is coal formed?

2. How is petroleum formed?

3. How is natural gas formed?

4. How many products are created from petroleum, and which is the most heavily consumed in the U.S.?

5. What is coke?

Thought Questions

Develop a complete answer for each of the following.

1. Explain why predictions and estimates of remaining fossil fuels are not completely reliable.

2. Discuss the environmental impacts of the production and use of coal.

3. Discuss the environmental impacts of the production and use of petroleum.

4. Compare the environmental impacts of natural gas with those of other fossil fuels, including tar sands and oil shales.

5. What are the major uses of petroleum? If the U.S. suddenly had its supply of oil cut in half, what uses would you eliminate (if any), and why?

6. Why have oil shales and tar sands played only a minor role as energy sources? Might this change in the future? Why or why not?

7. How have humans used fossil fuels throughout history?

Related Concepts

Describe the relationship. (There may be more than one.)

BETWEEN...	AND...
petroleum	oil shale
surface mining	acid drainage
petroleum	natural gas
OPEC	oil shortages of the 1970s
energy efficiency	CAFE standards

Suggested Activities

1. Read the Wall Street Journal for several weeks to follow gas prices and events in the world. What can you observe about how one influences the other?

2. Develop an energy conservation program for your community or campus. Include incentives to encourage people to participate.

3. Interview friends and family members about the 1973 OPEC oil embargo. What habits did they change? How did they feel about the situation?

4. Participate in an existing recycling program, or start your own. Find out how plastics (made from petroleum) are recycled. Recycle used motor oil.

5. If possible, begin walking, riding a bike, or taking public transportation to school or work instead of driving a car.

CHAPTER 13

Alternative Energy Resources

Chapter Outline

I. Describing Alternative Energy Resources

    A. Physical Boundaries

        1. Nuclear Energy

            a. Present and Future Use

            b. Advantages and Disadvantages

        2. Solar Energy

            a. Present and Future Use

            b. Advantages and Disadvantages

        3. Wind Power

            a. Present and Future Use

            b. Advantages and Disadvantages

        4. Hydropower

            a. Present and Future Use

            b. Advantages and Disadvantages

        5. Geothermal Power

            a. Present and Future Use

            b. Advantages and Disadvantages

        6. Ocean Power

            a. Present and Future Use

b. Advantages and Disadvantages

B. Biological Boundaries

　1. Biomass Energy

　　a. Present and Future Use

　　b. Advantages and Disadvantages

C. Social Boundaries

　1. Solid Waste

　　a. Present and Future Use

　　b. Advantages and Disadvantages

II. History of Management of Alternative Energy Resources

III. Future Management of Alternative Energy Resources

A. Prevent Overuse of Fossil Fuels Through Conservation

B. Protect Human Health and Environment

C. Preserve Living Systems

Learning Objectives

After learning the material in Chapter 13 you should be able to:

1. Identify eight alternative energy resources, summarize their current use and future use, and explain the advantages and disadvantages of each.

2. Identify the three major solar energy systems and their associated advantages/disadvantages.

3. List the limitations associated with capturing energy from the wind, and describe the idea behind "wind farms."

4. Describe the various methods of harnessing tidal power.

5. Describe the unique qualities of biomass energy conversion, and list the three different means by which this conversion occurs.

6. Briefly summarize the role that alternative energy resources have played historically.

7. Describe how alternative energy resources might be developed to complement and eventually supplant fossil fuels.

Did You Know...?

Bicycles transport more people in Asia alone than do all automobiles in the world combined.

Key Concepts

Read this summary of Chapter 13 and identify the important concepts discussed in the chapter.

Numerous energy resources may prove to be important alternatives to fossil fuels. These include nuclear energy, solar energy, wind power, hydropower, geothermal energy, ocean energy, and solid waste.

Nuclear energy, the energy contained within the nucleus of the atom, is released when an atom splits, or fissions, breaking apart into smaller atoms, releasing neutrons, and emitting heat energy. If the released neutrons bombard other fissionable atoms, a chain reaction results. Nuclear reactors are designed to sustain the fissioning process; they are powered by uranium-235 (U-235), a relatively rare fissionable uranium isotope (a form of an element that has the same number of protons but a different number of neutrons). A nuclear reactor core, housed within a containment vessel, heats water to produce steam that runs a turbine. While nuclear energy accounts for a modest proportion of the United States', and the world's, energy supply, its share of electric generation is significant, about 20% in the US and worldwide. France, Belgium, and several other countries rely on nuclear energy to produce as much as two-thirds of their electricity. The significant growth in the US nuclear industry during the 1970s and early 1980s has tapered off in recent years, primarily due to safety concerns and less-than-anticipated demand for electricity.

The sun, source of the energy vital for life on earth, can also provide energy for other purposes. Solar energy is used primarily for space and water heating. Passive solar systems incorporate design features of buildings and homes to capture the maximum amount of radiation from the sun during winter months and a minimum amount of radiation in the hot summer months. Only natural forces are used to distribute the heat. Active systems use fans or pumps driven by electricity to enhance the collection and distribution of the sun's heat. Solar energy may someday power electric generation on a significant basis. Photovoltaic cells generate electricity *directly* from sunlight. Atoms within these semiconductors absorb sunlight energy and liberate electrons, producing a direct electrical current. Advantages of solar power include: it exists everywhere (although intermittently in some areas), is nonpolluting, conserves natural resources, and is currently technologically available for widespread use. Disadvantages include: it is diffuse, and so has to be collected over large areas to make it practical to use, and is intermittent, and therefore requires some means of storage. Moreover, the initial cost of solar power for a home or small business can be quite high, although solar is less expensive than conventional fuels when life-cycle costs are determined.

The sun is also responsible for another potentially significant alternative energy resource. Because the sun warms different areas of the earth and the atmosphere in unequal amounts, regional pressure differences result which produce winds. Historically, wind energy was a fairly significant source of power. It is enjoying renewed interest because it is a safe, clean source of perpetual energy. Wind turbines clustered in favorable geographic locations make up wind farms. Disadvantages of wind power include the fact that it is variable and that it is site specific: it must be exploited in those areas where winds are reliable and strong enough to make the venture profitable (that is, areas where wind speed averages a minimum of 13 miles per hour).

Hydroelectric power results when water flows from the top of a dam to the bottom and strikes the blades of a turbine, which drives an electric generator. Most of the best sites for large-scale hydropower (areas with a steep, narrow gorge through which water falls) have already been developed. Increased emphasis is being put on developing smaller sites which produce less electrical energy but which are less environmentally damaging. Hydropower generates almost one fourth of the world's electricity, a contribution greater than that of nuclear power. Worldwide, it is responsible for the greatest proportion of electrical generating capacity of all renewable sources of energy. Advantages of hydropower include: it is nonpolluting and dams are multi-purpose, providing for recreational facilities, municipal water supplies, irrigation, and flood control, in addition to electric generation. Disadvantages include: dams destroy free-flowing rivers, flood lands, displace local peoples, ruin local streams and waterfalls, destroy fishing grounds in the area, cause siltation, and cause drastic changes in the composition of the biotic community.

Geothermal energy, heat generated by natural processes from the earth's vast subsurface storehouse of heat, includes dry steam, wet steam, and hot water deposits. Dry steam is the rarest and most preferred geothermal resource, and is also

135

the simplest and cheapest form for generating electricity. A hole is drilled into the dry steam reservoir and the released steam is filtered to eliminate solid materials and then piped directly to a turbine. Wet steam deposits, which consist of a mixture of steam, water droplets, and impurities such as salt, are more common than dry steam deposits but are also more difficult to use. The water is a wet steam deposit that is superheated; its temperature is far above the boiling point of water at normal atmospheric pressure. When a wet steam deposit is drilled and brought to the surface, a fraction of the water vaporizes instantly because of the decrease in pressure. The water-steam mixture is spun in a centrifuge to remove the steam, which is then purified and used to drive a turbine. Hot water deposits, such as those found in abundance in Iceland, are the most common type of geothermal energy. Geothermal energy does not play a major role in energy production globally, but twenty countries do realize a significant cumulative energy yield from this source. The major advantages of geothermal are: it is more environmentally benign than fossil fuels or nuclear power, and costs are moderate. Its major disadvantages area: deposits are nonrenewable on a human time scale, there are relatively few accessible deposits, substances dissolved in the steam and water may affect air and water quality, and emptying underground deposits may cause the overlying land to become unstable.

Ocean power, a relatively untapped energy resource, includes the power of tides, waves, deep ocean currents, and on- and off-shore winds, to name but a few. Of these, only tidal power has been used commercially. Barriers or dams are built across inlets or estuaries; the barriers house a series of electrical generating turbines. Depending on the system design, electricity can be generated during the ebb or flow tide.

While most alternative energy resources are physical in nature, one important source is not: the energy captured and stored by living organisms. Biomass is derived directly or indirectly from plant photosynthesis. One of the oldest and most versatile energy sources, its primary sources are forestry and wood processing residues; crop residues; animal waste products; garbage; and energy crops like trees, seaweed, and kelp. Biomass is particularly important in LDCs; in some areas, it is exploited to such a degree that forests and land health are threatened. Biomass can also be used to produce clean-burning alcohol fuels such as ethyl alcohol or ethanol. These fuels could serve as an important alternative to gasoline, both because they are renewable (gasoline supplies are finite) and because they are cleaner-burning, thus reducing pollution. A further use of biomass are the gases released by decaying plant matter and animal waste, called biogas. Methane is the chief component of biogas. Biogas can be captured and used as a boiler fuel; it is fairly common in some countries, notably China. The advantages of biomass are: it is clean, readily accessible, and fairly inexpensive. Disadvantages are: potential threat to land health when overexploited.

Solid wastes, a direct result of human activity, hold much potential as an energy resource. Using solid waste to produce energy (accomplished by burning refuse) is called trash conversion. Another source of energy derived from solid wastes is biogas. Biogas digesters are being installed in urban landfills with increasing regularity. Pipes drilled into landfills siphon the gas into storage tanks.

The exploitation of alternative sources, which may seem like a new and innovative development, is really an ancient practice. For centuries, humans have used solar radiation from the sun and heat from the earth and have harnessed the power of winds, water, and ocean tides. The recent (in historic terms) widespread availability of inexpensive supplies of oil, natural gas and coal, caused a decrease in the use of alternative sources. But declining oil reserves and increased environmental concerns associated with fossil fuels and nuclear power are spurring renewed interest in solar, wind power, hydrothermal power, and other alternatives.

Key Terms

active solar system

binding force

biomass

containment vessel

fission

geothermal energy

hydropower

isotope

nuclear energy

passive solar system

photovoltaic cell

reactor core

solar energy

solar pond

tidal power

trash conversion

wind power

wind turbine

Environmental Success Story

When most people imagine alternative ways of powering a vehicle, they think of methanol and ethanol, but what about vegetable oil? Louis Wichinski has turned this idea into reality by converting his 1979 Volkswagen Rabbit to run on vegetable oil. His car averages around 54 miles per gallon and gives off no toxic emissions such as sulfur dioxide or hydrocarbons, like gasoline does. Wichinski has found a way around the $2.60 per gallon cost for wholesale vegetable oil--his local diner and Burger King. He believes that other alternatives such as liquid propane, hydrogen, and butanol are less practical than vegetable oil. He says the only thing keeping the price high is that states such as New Mexico, Arizona, and Texas do not grow enough rapeseed, a great source of vegetable oil.

True/False

1. Electricity generated from nuclear power plants is significantly cheaper than energy generated from fossil fuels.　　T　　F

2. Although they once showed great promise, photovoltaic cells are no longer thought to be a useful technology.　　T　　F

3. After nuclear power, wind power is the second fastest growing energy source in the world.　　T　　F

4. Burning is the least efficient means of converting biomass to energy.　　T　　F

5. In the U.K., the tax on gasoline is greater than the cost of the gasoline itself.　　T　　F

Fill in the Blank

1. The isotope that fuels nuclear reactors is _____.

2. Passive solar systems rely on the natural forces of _____,
   _____, and _____.

3. The average minimum wind speed required for wind power systems is _____.

4. Three types of geothermal energy deposits are _____, _____,
   and _____.

5. The production of sugarcane produces a residue known as _____.

Multiple Choice

Choose the best answer.

1. All of the following are used as coolants in nuclear reactors except
   A. helium.
   B. uranium dioxide.
   C. heavy water.
   D. liquid metal.

2. A passive solar system can satisfy as much as _____ of a home's heating and
   cooling needs.
   A. 80%
   B. 90%
   C. 100%
   D. None of the above is true.

3. Which renewable source of energy produces the greatest proportion of electricity
   generating capacity worldwide?
   A. geothermal power
   B. solar power
   C. wind power
   D. hydropower

4. A potentially adverse environmental impact of large tidal power plants is
   A. land subsidence.
   B. reduced tidal current flow.
   C. increased tidal range.
   D. both b & c.

5. Which of the following energy sources is NOT primarily composed of biomass?
   A. agrifuel
   B. ethanol
   C. biogas
   D. crop-residue

Short Answer

1. What is the result when an atom is bombarded by free neutron?

2. What is deuterium oxide? What is its role in producing nuclear energy?

3. What is a power tower?

4. What is trash conversion?

5. What is a carbon tax?

Thought Questions

Develop a complete answer for each of the following.

1. Describe the process used to prepare Uranium-235 for use in a nuclear reactor. Why is U-235, a relatively rare isotope, used instead of a more common form?

2. Compare the use of nuclear energy in the U.S. in the 1970s (before the OPEC oil embargo) and its use today. How does the U.S.'s use of nuclear energy compare with that of the rest of the world?

3. Explain the major arguments for and against the use of nuclear energy.

4. Describe two types of energy-producing systems that are primarily solar driven. How are they different? How are they similar? What are the advantages and disadvantages of each?

5. Why isn't wind power used as a major energy source today? Why is it less commonly used today than it was a century ago? Do you expect use of wind power to increase or decrease in the future? Why?

6. What is refuse-derived fuel? What problems have accompanied its use to generate electricity?

7. Compared to fossil fuels, are alternative energy sources better? Worse? The same? Explain your answer.

Related Concepts

Describe the relationship.   (There may be more than one.)

BETWEEN...	AND...
active solar system	passive solar systems
hydroelectric production in MDCs	hydroelectric production in LDCs
watershed management	large-scale dams

Did You Know . . . ?

Solar powered calculators are the best-selling solar device sold in the United States.

Suggested Activities

1. Find a solar heating system and discover how it works.

2. Do you know where the electricity you use in your home comes from? Determine if your local utility company produces electricity from any alternative sources.

3. Use daylight whenever possible. Many tasks—reading, writing, studying—can be done by the light of a window.

UNIT FOUR

AN ENVIRONMENTAL TRIAD

CHAPTER 14

Air Resources: The Atmosphere

Chapter Outline

I. Describing Air Resources

   A. Physical and Biological Boundaries

      1. What Is the Atmosphere?

      2. How Does the Atmosphere Help to Maintain the Earth's Climate?

   B. Social Boundaries

      1. What Is Air Pollution?

         a. Global Warming

         b. Acid Precipitation

         c. Photochemical Smog

         d. Stratospheric Ozone Depletion

         e. Indoor Air Pollution

            1. Formaldehyde

            2. Radon 222

            3. Tobacco Smoke

            4. Asbestos

         f. Airborne Toxins

      2. What Factors Affect Air Pollution Levels?

143

a. Weather

b. Topography

c. Temperature Inversions

II. History of Management of Air Resources

    A. What Is the Clean Air Act?

        1. Setting Emission Standards

        2. Meeting Emission Standards

    B. How Did the Clean Air Act Affect Air Quality in the United States?

    C. What Are the Provisions of the 1990 Amendment to the Clean Air Act?

    D. What Initiatives Are Being Undertaken to Improve Air Quality in the United States?

    E. What Initiatives Are Being Undertaken to Improve Global Air Quality?

III. Future Management of Air Resources

    A. Prevent the Abuse of Air Resources Through Conservation

    B. Protect Human Health and the Environment

    C. Preserve Living Systems

Learning Objectives

After learning the material in Chapter 14 you should be able to:

1. Define air and the atmosphere, and explain their importance to life on earth.

2. Explain primary and secondary pollution.

3. Discuss the major sources and effects of the most significant primary air pollutants.

4. Explain the environmental and health dangers of two secondary pollutants, acid precipitation and ground level ozone.

5. Describe the effects of weather and topography on air pollution.

6. Discuss the greenhouse effect and stratospheric ozone depletion.

7. Explain the status of U.S. air quality regulations and standards.

8. Make recommendations for improving the world's air resources.

Did You Know . . . ?

One hundred percent of the United States' energy needs could be supplied by wind power.

Key Concepts

Read this summary of Chapter 14 and identify the important concepts discussed in the chapter.

The atmosphere is all the gaseous matter that surrounds the earth. The atmosphere plays an important role in influencing climate, the long-term weather pattern of a particular region. Atmospheric gases allow some of the incoming solar radiation to pass through the atmosphere, but trap heat that would otherwise be reradiated back toward space. The greenhouse gases are essential to maintaining the conditions necessary for life on earth, but increased levels of them can lead to global warming.

Any substance present in or released to the atmosphere that adversely affects human health or the environment is considered an air pollutant. Pollution levels are affected by weather and topography. In the 1970s efforts at cleaning up air pollution in the United States focused on primary pollutants. Currently, increased attention is being given to six air pollution issues that pose a particular threat: global warming, acid precipitation, photochemical smog, stratospheric ozone depletion, indoor air pollution, and airborne toxics.

Global warming is expected to cause changes in the world climate if not stopped in time. However, not everyone agrees that global warming is actually occurring or that it is being caused by human activity.

Damage caused by acid precipitation is widespread, both in the United States and globally. Photochemical smog is a serious problem in urban areas worldwide.

Ozone in the stratosphere plays a critical role in protecting the earth from harmful ultraviolet radiation; its depletion is expected to increase cancer rates and decrease marine productivity. Indoor air pollutants and airborne toxics also pose a significant threat to human health and the environment.

In the United States air pollution is regulated chiefly by the Clean Air Act, first passed in 1963 and amended in 1970, 1977, and 1990.

Key Terms

acid precipitation

acid surge

airborne toxins

air pollutant

albedo

ambient concentration

atmosphere

chlorofluorocarbon

emission standards

emissivity

global warming

greenhouse effect

mesosphere

ozone

photochemical reaction

photochemical smog

primary pollutant

radon 222

rain shadow effect

secondary pollutant

stratosphere

thermosphere

troposphere

Environmental Success Story

Lynda Draper became alarmed when a GE refrigerator repairman asked her to open her kitchen window so coolant could be vented. She became infuriated, telling the man what she knows of the ozone-destroying CFCs that were drifting out her window into the upper atmosphere. After this, she became a major force, taking on GE and getting them to phase out their CFCs by launching a $450 million refrigerator repair program. She has become a symbol of consumer awareness by helping to get other companies as well to change their policies dealing with CFCs.

True/False

1. Air is composed primarily of oxygen.   T   F

2. Areas with a low albedo, such as polar ice caps and deserts,   T   F
    reflect more energy than they absorb.

3. Average global temperature is about 59°F.   T   F

4. Secondary pollutants are those that are released to the atmosphere in relatively small quantities. T F

5. The primary component of photochemical smog is ozone. T F

Fill in the Blank

1. Infrared ray-absorbing gases in the atmosphere are often referred to as

   _____ .

2. Short, intense periods of acid deposition in lakes and streams are called   .

3. Older industrial cities that rely on coal for generating electricity are likely to suffer from _____ .

4. The phenomenon that causes one side of a mountain to be damaged by pollution while the other side remains unharmed is known as _____ .

5. Label the diagram of the atmosphere. [Figure 14-1, with scores where labels would be]

Multiple Choice

Choose the best answer.

1. The atmospheric level in which weather occurs is the
   A. mesosphere.
   B. stratosphere.
   C. thermosphere.
   D. troposphere.

2. The capacity of a surface to radiate heat is its
   A. albedo.
   B. emissivity.
   C. radiational effect.
   D. greenhouse effect.

3. Which of the following is NOT true of acid precipitation?
   A. It occurs in the form of rain, snow, fog, mist or dust.
   B. It has a pH of 5.5 or lower.
   C. Its low pH results primarily from sulfuric and carbonic acid.
   D. None of the above is true.

4. All of the following are major indoor air pollutants except
   A. carbon dioxide.
   B. formaldehyde.
   C. asbestos.
   D. radon 222.

5. Ozone is an air pollutant in which of the following places?
   A. indoors
   B. troposphere
   C. stratosphere
   D. All of the above are true.

Short Answer

1. List the components of clean, dry air.

2. What are the six primary air pollutants?

3. What are the major indoor air pollutants?

4. What are the causes of temperature inversions?

5. What is the largest unregulated source of air pollution in the U.S.?

Thought Questions

Develop a complete answer for each of the following.

1. Explain the importance of the greenhouse effect in maintaining life on earth. List the causes of increased greenhouse gases and describe the effects that may result.

2. What evidence exists that global warming is already occurring? What are the arguments and uncertainties that point to the contrary? Discuss the general agreements (the "greenhouse knowns") among the scientific community.

3. Discuss the causes and effects of acid precipitation. Why is it such a widespread problem? What are the political problems associated with regulating it?

4. Explain the "split personality" of ozone. Include in your answer a discussion of the effects of ozone on human health.

5. What are CFCs and how are they used? What is their impact on the environment?

149

6. Discuss the effects of indoor air pollution. What factors make this a difficult type of pollution to control?

7. Describe the history of the air quality legislation in the U.S. Has it been effective? Why or why not?

Related Concepts

Describe the relationship. (There may be more than one.)

BETWEEN...	AND...
urban heat islands	global warming
soil composition	acid precipitation
topography & weather	air pollution
airborne toxics	water pollution
standard of living	air quality in the U.S.

Did You Know . . . ?

In 1990, the ozone hole over Antarctica was the width of the United States and the height of Mount Everest.

Suggested Activities

1. Measure radon levels in your home. Refer to EPA guidelines in deciding whether and how quickly to take action based on your test results.

2. Stop smoking and discourage smoking in your home.

3. If you have your car air conditioner serviced, choose a car repair shop that uses CFC recycling equipment.

CHAPTER 15

Water Resources: The Hydrosphere

Chapter Outline

I. Describing Water Resources

   A. Biological Boundaries

   B. Physical Boundaries

      1. How Much Clean Fresh Water Is There?

      2. How Is Water Classified?

         a. Fresh Water

            1. Surface Water

            2. Groundwater

         b. Marine and Coastal Resources

            1. Estuaries

            2. Coastal Wetlands

            3. Coral Reefs

            4. Continental Shelves

   C. Social Boundaries

      1. How Do We Use Water?

      2. How Do Water Consumption Patterns Vary Worldwide?

      3. What Kinds of Water Pollution Are There?

         a. Organic Wastes

b. Disease-Causing Wastes

c. Plant Nutrients

d. Sediments

e. Toxic and Hazardous Substances

f. Persistent Substances

g. Radioactive Substances

h. Heat

II. History of Management of Water Resources

A. How Have Humans Managed Water Resources in the Past?

B. How Have Water Resources Been Managed in the United States?

1. New York

2. Los Angeles

3. New Orleans

C. What Legislation Protects the Nation's Water Resources?

1. Safe Drinking Water Act

2. Federal Water Pollution Control Act

D. How Are Drinking Water Supplies Treated?

E. How Is Wastewater Treated?

F. What Problems Surround the Use of Water Worldwide?

G. How Is Groundwater Managed?

H. How Are Fresh Surface Waters Managed?

I. How Are Marine Waters Managed?

III. Future Management of Water Resources

A. Prevent Overuse Through Conservation

B. Protect Human Health and the Environment

C. Preserve Living Systems

Learning Objectives

After learning the material in Chapter 15 you should be able to:

1. List properties of water that enable it to support life.

2. Identify how water resources are classified and briefly describe each classification.

3. Describe worldwide water consumption patterns.

4. Identify eight broad categories of water pollution.

5. Describe how people have managed water resources in the past.

6. Describe how both drinking water supplies and wastewater are treated.

7. List some of the current threats to groundwater, lakes, rivers, and marine waters.

Did You Know . . . ?

Twenty percent of all toilets in the United States are leaking right now. (One leaking toilet wastes over 22,000 gallons of water.)

Key Concepts

Read this summary of Chapter 15 and identify the important concepts discussed in the chapter.

Water is synonymous with life. It is the largest constituent of living organisms, and it is also a habitat in which life evolved on earth and exists today. All organisms, including humans, are intricately bound to the hydrological (water) cycle.

Most of the earth's water (97 percent) is salty. Three quarters of the remaining fresh water is locked in polar ice caps and glaciers, and one quarter is found underground as groundwater. Only .5 percent of all water in the world is found in lakes, rivers, streams, and the atmosphere.

Water is classified as either salt (marine) water or fresh water depending on its salt content. Fresh water is found on land in two basic forms: surface water and groundwater. Surface waters include all bodies of water that are usually recharged by runoff from precipitation. Surface water ecosystems include both standing water habitats, which are relatively closed ecosystems with well-defined boundaries, and running water habitats, which are continuously moving currents of water.

The United States contains about 20 times more groundwater than surface water. Groundwater percolates downward through the soil after precipitation or from surface water and is stored in an aquifer. Aquifers can range in size from a few square miles to thousands of square miles. Groundwater is the major source of drinking water in about two-thirds of the states. In addition, it helps to maintain water levels and the productivity of streams, lakes, rivers, wetlands, bays, and estuaries.

The world's oceans support over half of the world's biomass, and are one huge living system. Currents move water around the continents and across the open sea, continually circulating nutrients washed in from the land. The interaction of the oceans and the atmosphere affects heat distribution, weather patterns, and concentrations of atmospheric gases throughout the world. Four biologically productive ecosystems are responsible for most of the oceans' primary production: estuaries, coastal wetlands, coral reefs, and offshore continental shelves.

We use water for many purposes, but globally, agriculture is the single greatest drain on water supplies. Water uses may be consumptive or nonconsumptive. Nonconsumptive uses remove water, use it, and return it to its original source. Consumptive uses remove water from one place in the hydrological cycle and return it to another.

Water pollution can be divided into eight general categories: organic wastes, disease-causing wastes, plant nutrients, toxic and hazardous substances, persistent substances, sediments, radioactive substances, and heat. Some of these categories overlap. One source may be responsible for more than one type of pollutant, or one pollutant may fit into more than one category. Pollutants can also act together synergistically. Many water systems are assaulted by pollutants from all eight categories, and cleaning up all of them can be extremely difficult.

Humans have always settled close to waterways, which supplied water for drinking and irrigation, the transportation of goods, and the dilution of wastes. Water management and the development of civilization have often gone hand in hand. Europeans who emigrated to the New World found a seemingly endless supply of clean water and could not imagine that water could ever be a problem. However, as populations increased, water pollution became a threat to human health and the environment.

In the United States, two pieces of legislation—the Safe Drinking Water Act of 1974 and the Federal Water Pollution Control Act of 1972—determine how water is managed. The Safe Drinking Water Act set national drinking water standards, called maximum contaminant levels (MCLs) for pollutants that might adversely affect human health. It also established standards to protect groundwater from hazardous wastes injected into the soil. The Federal Water Pollution Control Act, commonly called the Clean Water Act, divided pollutants into three classes: toxic, conventional, and unconventional. It established standards industries and sewage treatment plants must follow when discharging certain classes of waste.

Wastewater can be handled in several different ways. In rural and some suburban areas with suitable soils, sewage and wastewater from each home are usually discharged into a septic tank. Wastewater in urban areas must be transported from a variety of sites to sewage treatment plants. Combined sewer systems carry both wastewater and rainwater, and are designed to protect the treatment plant. During storms, the combined flow may bypass the treatment plant and enter a receiving stream. Separate sewer systems carry wastewater and rainwater in separate systems. They can be costly, but protect the receiving stream from pollutants.

When wastewater enters a sewage treatment plant, it usually goes through a multistage process including physical and biological processes to reduce it to an acceptable effluent. Constructing and operating effective sewage plants is expensive. Currently, most of the expense must be borne by local authorities, and for many towns and municipalities, the costs of upgrading are prohibitive.

Fresh and marine waters worldwide are besieged by numerous threats. Contamination by pollutants is a threat to all water sources. Many underground aquifers experience overdraft. Toxic pollutants and accelerated eutrophication are serious threats to the nation's lakes. Threats to rivers include dams, diversions, and channelization. All of our coastal ecosystems are under severe stress. Until recently, little thought was given to effectively managing and preserving marine environments.

Key Terms

abyssal zone

aquifer

biological oxygen demand (B.O.D.)

combined sewer system

desalination

epilimnion

euphotic zone

eutrophic

groundwater

hypolimnion

land subsidence

limnetic zone

littoral zone

neritic zone

oligotrophic

overdraft

pelagic zone

profundal zone

running water habitat

runoff

separate sewer system

septic tank

standing water habitat

thermal stratification

thermocline

water mining

water table

watershed

Environmental Success Story

As a lobsterer living in Maine, George Whidden has a close relationship with the ocean. Recently, he has become very concerned about the condition that oceans are in. In reaction to his observations, Whidden organized the Coalition to Cease Ocean Dumping. He explains that the ocean has been good to him, and he is concerned that his grandchildren will be left with a cesspool. He explains this by telling of a "dolphin goin' belly up" and a dead whale with its skin peeled back "like sunburn, and not for lack of Coppertone."

True or False

1. Only about 3% of the earth's water is fresh water.   T   F

2. Photosynthesis occurs in the profundal zone only in   T   F
   summer.

3. Aquifers supply drinking water for half of the U.S.   T   F
   population.

4. Secondary treatment of wastewater is usually about 85%   T   F
   effective.

5. Groundwater withdrawal has tripled since the 1950s.   T   F

Fill in the Blank

1. Cold, deep lakes with a high O_2 content are called _ _ _ lakes.

2. Label the layers of thermal stratification. [Figure 15-3]

3. Label the ocean zones. [Figure 15-7]

4. The amount of oxygen needed to decompose the organic matter in water is called _____ .

5. _____ treatment of wastewater is a biological process.

Multiple Choice

Choose the best answer.

1. Most of the earth's fresh water is contained in
   A. lakes, rivers, and streams .
   B. the atmosphere.
   C. aquifers.
   D. None of the above is true.

2. The shallow area near the shore of a lake where rooted plants grow is the
   A. profundal zone.
   B. limnetic zone.
   C. littoral zone.
   D. pelagic zone.

3. Phytoplankton grow most abundantly in the
   A. pelagic zone.
   B. littoral zone.
   C. euphotic zone.
   D. neritic zone.

4. The test used to determine if water is likely to be contaminated with disease-causing organisms looks for the presence of
   A. coliforms.
   B. nitrosamines.
   C. giardiasis.
   D. algal blooms.

5. A feature of tertiary treatment of wastewater is
   A. activated carbon absorption.
   B. activated sludge.
   C. removal of undissolved solids.
   D. None of the above is true.

Short Answer

1. What is a watershed?

2. List the defining characteristics of eutrophic lakes.

3. What are confirmed aquifers and confined aquifers?

4. Define *effluent*.

5. What chemicals are commonly added to drinking water supplies and why?

Thought Questions

Develop a complete answer for each of the following.

1. Discuss the human health and environmental problems associated with water consumption worldwide.

2. List and briefly describe the effects of the eight types of water pollution.

3. Explain the U.S. legislation designed to protect water quality.

4. Describe the process of wastewater treatment. Include in your answer a comparison of combined and separate sewer systems. What occurs at each stage (primary, secondary, tertiary) of treatment?

5. What is the importance of the U.S.' groundwater resources? What are the major threats to them?

Related Concepts

Describe the relationship. (There may be more than one.)

BETWEEN...	AND...
seasons	thermal stratification
riffles and pools	running water habitats
organic waste	eutrophication
irrigation	channelization
erosion control	Palmiter method of river restoration

Did You Know . . . ?

Americans use 1/3 more water during the summer months than any other part of the year.

Suggested Activities

1. Contact your water company to ask for the most recent analysis of the compound and chemicals found in your drinking water, or obtain your own water analysis. Compare your results with the national limits set by the EPA.

2. Does your county or town have its own water quality standards? Find out what they are and how they are enforced.

3. Investigate the effect of oil spills on aquatic habitats. Examples of recent spills you may want to study are the Prince Edward Sound, Alaska spill (Exxon *Valdez*), or the Persian Gulf spills which occurred during the 1991 expulsion of Iraqi troops from Kuwait.

4. Look for and eliminate leaks around your home.

CHAPTER 16

Soil Resources: The Lithosphere

Chapter Outline

3. Reliance on Fossil Fuels

4. Reliance on Synthetic Agricultural Chemicals

5. Groundwater Depletion

6. Overirrigation

7. Loss of Genetic Diversity

8. Socioeconomic Concerns

C. How Has the U.S. Government Responded to the Farm Crisis?

1. The 1985 Farm Bill

2. LISA -- Low-input Sustainable Agriculture

D. What Is Sustainable Agriculture?

1. Measures to Prevent Excessive Soil Erosion

2. Measures to Restore and Maintain Soil Fertility

3. Organic Farming

4. Polyculture and Perennial Polyculture

III. Future Management

A. Prevent Overuse Through Conservation

B. Protect Human Health and the Environment

C. Preserve Living Systems

Learning Objectives

After learning the material in Chapter 16 you should be able to:

1. Describe the major components of soil and explain how soil is formed.

2. Explain the meaning of the statement, "Soil teems with life."

3. Differentiate between the distinct layers that make up a soil horizon.

4. List the major uses for land and describe how land use affects agriculture.

5. Compare conventional and sustainable agriculture practices.

6. List the environmental problems associated with high-input (conventional) agriculture.

7. Discuss methods to prevent soil erosion and maintain soil fertility.

Did You Know ... ?

Two hundred and fifty-three plant species in the United States are at risk of becoming extinct in five years.

Key Concepts

Read this summary of Chapter 16 and identify the important concepts discussed in the chapter.

Soil, the topmost layer of the earth's surface in which plants grow, is an ecosystem composed of abiotic and biotic components, such as inorganic chemicals, air, water, decaying organic material, and living organisms. As such, it is subject to the dynamics that operate in all ecosystems. Humus, which consists of partially decomposed organic matter, helps to retain water and to maintain a high nutrient content, thus enabling soil to remain fertile. Soil fertility refers to the soil's mineral and organic content, while soil productivity refers to its ability to sustain life, especially vegetation. Every teaspoon of soil contains billions of beneficial organisms that help maintain soil fertility.

Soil varies in texture, structure, and fertility. Soil texture is the way the soil feels. Soil structure refers to the way soil particles clump together to form larger clumps, or peds. Scientists typically recognize ten major soil orders and an estimated 100,000 soil types.

Soil is a product of the physical, chemical, and biological interactions in specific locations. Five interacting factors work together to form soil: parent material, climate, topography, living organisms, and time. It may take hundreds or thousands of years for a mature soil to develop; it may take 10,000 years to form a layer of soil one foot thick.

As soils develop, they form distinct horizontal layers called soil horizons, each of which has a characteristic color, texture, structure, acidity, and composition. In general, soils have from three to five major horizons. These horizons include the O horizon (surface litter), the A horizon (topsoil), the E horizon (zone of leaching), the B horizon (containing minerals) and the C horizon (mostly parent material). A set of soil horizons is called a soil profile.

The way in which a particular piece of land is used is known as its land use. Depending on the soil type and the terrain, there may be many potential uses for a specific parcel of land. The use to which a piece of land is put can have immediate and long-lasting effects on the soil's resources. Worldwide, expanding urbanization poses a long-term threat to soil resources. An even greater threat to soil fertility and conservation is erosion. Erosion by wind and water is a natural process, and when undisturbed, soil is usually replaced faster than it erodes. Soil disturbed by human activity, however, can be eroded faster than it is replaced. Because soil takes so long to form, eroded soil is, in terms of the human life span, irreplaceable.

In the United States no land use has been more important historically than agriculture. When the Europeans first arrived on the North American continent, they cleared seemingly inexhaustible forest for farmlands. As land became increasingly scarce and the soils in some areas became less productive, settlers began to move westward. The rich grassland soils of the Great Plains produced large yields for years, but soil fertility gradually declined. In 1931 a severe drought combined with intense cultivation of unsuitable crops combined to produce the Dust Bowl, a period of extensive wind erosion.

In the 1950s and 1960s agricultural production was raised by the use of high inputs of chemicals, large machinery, and hybrid strains of crops. But high-input, or conventional, agriculture can cause serious problems, including soil degradation, soil erosion, reliance on fossil fuels, reliance on agrichemicals, groundwater depletion, overirrigation, loss of genetic diversity, and socioeconomic concerns.

U.S. agriculture has gradually moved from subsistence farming, with its small, family-owned farms into agribusiness, in which large commercial farms are owned by corporations. For the most part, the U.S. Department of Agriculture and government programs have supported the trend toward highly specialized, energy-intensive, and environmentally questionable farming practices.

The search for effective methods to protect the soil and restore its fertility is resulting in the development of various systems of alternative or sustainable agriculture, which both sustain and protect the soil and its productivity. These methods include tilling the soil as little as possible, using few pesticides, tilling the soil at angles and places to reduce erosion, and growing a variety of crops instead of just one. Of all forms of agriculture, organic farms most closely resemble natural systems.

Key Terms

agribusiness

agrichemical

conservation tillage

contour plowing

contour terracing

cover crop

crop rotation

green manure

high-input agriculture

humus

integrated pest management (IPM)

land use

low-input sustainable agriculture (LISA)

parent material

perennial polyculture

ridge tilling

salinization

soil fertility

soil horizon

soil loss tolerance level (T-value)

soil productivity

soil profile

strip cropping

sustainable agriculture

tilth

topsoil

trickle drip irrigation

Environmental Success Story

A Toledo, Ohio company has found an innovative way of dealing with the sludge that comes from municipal wastewater treatment plants in the area. N-Viro Energy Systems Ltd. has more than 40 plants that process sludge to be used throughout North America by farmers, landscapers, land reclaimers, and landfill operators. The product is called N-Viro soil because it looks and performs like natural soil. This new soil is cleansed of disease-causing organisms, but the organisms that benefit farmers are retained. Although it took the company only two and a half years to expand to over 40 operations, it is sure to grow even more due to the high demand for environmentally sensitive products.

True or False

1. Soil fertility refers to the ability of a soil to sustain life (e.g., vegetation).   T   F

2. Loams are the best soil types for growing most crops.   T   F

3. In the days of the Dust Bowl, soil was being depleted at the fastest rate in U.S. history.   T   F

4. Water accounts for two-thirds of the erosion on U.S. farmland.   T   F

5. About 10% of America's farmers are using organic farming techniques.   T   F

Fill in the Blank

1. The mineral and organic content of soil determines its _____.

2. The arrangement of soil particles into lumps or crumbs is known as ____.

3. Label the soil horizons in the figure below. [Figure 16-4, without labels]

4. Raw mineral material from which soil is formed is called __.

5. The _____ describes the tons of soil per acre per year that a given area can lose through erosion without a loss of fertility.

Multiple choice

Choose the best answer.

1. Silt particles
   A. are less than 0.00008" in diameter.
   B. feel like flour when rubbed between the fingers.
   C. are sticky when wet.
   D. All of the above are true.

2. The soil layer in which dissolved minerals accumulate is the
   A. *A* horizon.
   B. *B* horizon.
   C. *E* horizon.
   D. *O* horizon.

3. The zone of leaching is also called the
   A. *A* horizon.
   B. *B* horizon.
   C. *C* horizon.
   D. *E* horizon.

4. The first European settlers in North America used farming techniques that included
   A. continual cropping.
   B. crop rotation.
   C. irrigation.
   D. None of the above is true.

5. A technique that is designed to reduce erosion on sloped farmland is
   A. contour plowing.
   B. trickle drip irrigation.
   C. crop rotation.
   D. ridge tilling.

Short Answer

1. Describe the abiotic composition of soil.

2. List and describe the three soil categories based on texture.

3. What are the five interacting factors that form soil?

4. What are the two major causes of agricultural soil erosion?

5. What is a perennial polyculture?

Thought Questions

Develop a complete answer for each of the following.

1. In a temperate deciduous forest, a stream cuts through the exposed bedrock of a small valley. Describe the processes by which soil may form here.

2. Which land uses are the biggest threats to soil fertility and conservation in the United States? How can land use planning help?

3. Discuss the factors and events that led to the Dust Bowl.

4. What changes occurred in American agriculture during the 1950s and 1960s? Discuss the continuing effects of these changes on the environment.

5. What is sustainable agriculture? Where and how is it being practiced today, and with what results?

6. Discuss how the U.S. government has responded to the farm crisis.

Related Concepts

Describe the relationship. (There may be more than one.)

BETWEEN...	AND...
Dust Bowl	soil conservation
soil erosion	loss of wildlife habitat
irrigation	groundwater depletion
1985 Farm Bill	erosion
LISA	organic farming

Did You Know . . . ?

Before pesticides were widely used, farmers often lost about 33 percent of their crops to pests. However, with the use of pesticides today, 33 percent of the crops are still lost to pests.

Suggested Activities

1. Find out what kinds of crops are grown in your part of the country. Locate the Soil Conservation Service in your area and find out what kinds of conservation techniques are recommended.

2. If you have a vegetable garden, try using biological pest controls and other alternatives to pesticides.

3. Compare the appearance and taste of organically grown fruits and vegetables with those that are conventionally grown.

UNIT FIVE

AN ENVIRONMENTAL PANDORA'S BOX

CHAPTER 17

Mineral Resources

Chapter Outline

I. Describing the Resource

    A. Physical and Biological Boundaries

        1. How Did the Earth Form and How Does It Change?

        2. What Are Minerals?

        3. How Are Minerals Classified?

        4. How Are Minerals Formed?

        5. Where Are Minerals Found?

    B. Social Boundaries

        1. How Are Minerals Used?

        2. How Is the Size of Mineral Deposits Estimated?

        3. How Long Will Mineral Reserves Last?

        4. What Are the Steps in the Mining Process?

            a. Location

            b. Extraction

c. Processing

d. Summary: Environmental Impact of Mining

II. History of Management

A. What Is the Historical Significance of Minerals?

B. How Do Economic Factors Affect Mineral Production and Consumption?

C. What Is the International Minerals Industry?

D. How Is Seabed Mining Overseen?

E. How Does the United States Manage Mineral Supplies?

1. Domestic Mineral Supplies

2. Imported Mineral Supplies

F. What Can We Do to Conserve Mineral Resources?

III. Future Management

A. Prevent Overuse Through Conservation

B. Protect Human Health and the Environment

C. Preserve Living Systems

Learning Objectives

After learning the material in Chapter 17 you should be able to:

1. Describe how igneous and sedimentary rocks are formed.

2. Define "mineral resources" and list the three ways in which these resources naturally occur.

3. Distinguish between proven and recoverable mineral resources.

4. Describe the steps and environmental consequences of the mining process.

5. Identify the various ways in which ore can be classified.

6. Explain the different classifications of mineral availability and explain why the "ultimately recoverable resource" percentage is the best indicator of the total amount of a given mineral that will likely be available for future use.

7. Compare and contrast the various means of extracting mineral resources, and identify the human and environmental problems associated with each.

8. Compare mineral availability and use in more-developed and less-developed countries.

Did You Know . . . ?

Polystyrene foam cups are completely non-biodegradable.

Key Concepts

Read this summary of Chapter 17 and identify the important concepts discussed in the chapter.

Although inorganic matter may seem to be unchanging, it has actually undergone much change and transformation since the earth began, and is still changing. Igneous rock is formed through volcanic activity, and sedimentary rock is formed by the deposit of small bits of matter carried by rain or wind and then compacted and cemented to form rock.

The earth consists of several different layers. At the center is a dense, metallic core, which is surrounded by a mantle. The outer layer is called the crust, and contains the mineral deposits exploited by humans.

Minerals are nonliving, naturally occurring substances with a limited range in chemical composition and with an orderly atomic arrangement. A mineral may occur in one of three forms: as a single element, a compound of elements, or an aggregate of elements and compounds. Each mineral's unique chemical formula determines its physical properties, such as strength, insulating or sealing capacity, electrical conductivity, or beauty. Minerals are broadly classified as fuels or nonfuels. Nonfuels are further classified as metallic or nonmetallic. Metals are sometimes classified by their abundance or scarcity in the earth's crust. Abundant metals make up more than .1 percent of the earth's crust, by weight. Scarce metals make up less than .1 percent of the earth's crust.

Minerals can be found everywhere, but they are not evenly distributed throughout the earth's crust. Many scientists believe the distribution of mineral deposits is related to the past and present movement of the earth's tectonic plates. Additionally, deposits of one mineral are often mixed with deposits of others. Mineral deposits are dispersed by weathering and erosion. They are formed by chemical separation and also affected by gravity.

To be useful, a mineral must be profitable to extract. Where a concentration is high enough to make mining economically feasible, the mineral deposit is known as an ore. Some nations are mineral-rich and others are mineral-poor.

Minerals are used in many different ways: in steel production, manufacturing, industrial processes, fertilizers, and construction. The greatest share of mineral resources is consumed by the more developed countries. MDCs, with about one quarter of the world's population, use about three-quarters of the global production of nonfuel minerals. Global demand for most major minerals is expected to rise significantly as the human population continues to grow rapidly and societies continue to rely on mineral resources to support rising standards of living. MDCs rely on about 80 minerals; three-quarters of these either exist in abundant supply to meet our anticipated needs or can be replaced by existing substitutes. Critical minerals are those considered essential to a nation's economic activity; strategic minerals are those considered essential to a nation's defense. At present, there are no suitable alternatives for critical or strategic minerals.

An estimate of the total sum of a mineral found in the earth is called the resource base; this estimate is highly theoretical. A mineral deposit that can be extracted profitably with current technology is called a proven reserve or economic resource. Subeconomic resources are reserves that have been discovered but cannot yet be extracted at a profit at current prices or with current technology. An estimate of the total amount of a given mineral that is likely to be available for future use is called the ultimately recoverable resource. This estimate is based on known reserves, plus assumptions about discovery rates, future costs, market factors, and future advances in extraction and processing technologies. It is unlikely that mineral resources will ever become exhausted. As reserves become depleted, the cost is likely to rise. High prices and high demand encourage more exploration and lead to the discovery of more ores.

Mining includes three major steps: location, extraction, and processing. All can adversely affect human and environmental health. Modern exploration relies on knowledge of geology and the use of sophisticated equipment. Most high-grade ores have already been identified and exploited. The ocean floor and Antarctica hold real potential for profitable mining, but because they are global commons, disputes over mining claims are a problem. Extraction is the process of separating a mineral ore from the surrounding rock in which it is embedded. Ore may be extracted by surface mining or subsurface mining techniques. Extraction degrades the environment by promoting erosion and siltation, rearranging the layers of soil, leaving tailings containing hazardous substances, and polluting water. Extraction is also hazardous to human health. Processing consists of separating the mineral from the ore in which it is held and concentrating and refining the separated mineral. Processing ores causes soil and water pollution, and also affects human health.

Market supply and demand determine the price of minerals. Supply and demand, in turn, are influenced by the needs and uses of society, technological constraints, economic forces, and resource scarcity. Scarcity is related to political, economic, and technical factors, not actual reserves. Mineral prices tend to fluctuate wildly in the short term, but over time the economic value attached to commodity exports such as minerals has fallen relative to the value of manufactured goods. Mineral-exporting nations, particularly LDCs, must sell increasing amounts of minerals to pay for imports such as tractors and fertilizers.

In the United States the development of domestic mineral deposits on public land is governed by the Mining Law of 1872, which grants title to certain public lands as long as certain criteria are met. Some mineral deposits are currently governed under the 1920 Mineral Leasing Act, which allows private individuals and companies to lease the rights to develop these resources. In the 1990s the debate between mineral development and preservation on the public lands has intensified. The focus of the debate will probably shift to Alaska, which contains sizable reserves of many important nonfuel minerals, but also much wilderness. The United States imports most strategic and critical minerals. To guard against shortages, it stockpiles important minerals.

Minerals can be conserved by finding substitutes for those that are in short supply, reusing products and materials, and recycling materials. Substitutes are materials that can replace traditional materials and have more of a desired property. They generally use less metals and other minerals than traditional materials, or use minerals that have not been widely used. The "throwaway mentality" of American society has caused us to recycle significantly less than we are able to. This attitude must change if we are to conserve material resources and reduce solid waste.

Key Terms

abundant metal

advanced material

area strip mining

contour strip mining

critical mineral

extraction

ferrous metal

igneous rock

magma

metamorphic rock

mineral

nonferrous metal

open pit surface mining

ore

overburden

processing

proven reserve

resource base

scarce metal

sedimentary rock

strategic mineral

subeconomic resource

subsurface mining

surface mining

tailings

ultimately recoverable resource

Environmental Success Story

To guard against the curiosity of humans, gates have been used for years to protect caves and the creatures that live in them. Until recently, however, none has been able to keep humans out while also serving the needs of the cave-dwelling animals. Recently, Roy Powers has been recognized for his great designs of cave gates. He has helped design or install around 60 gates at cave entrances throughout the United States and has even survived a lightning strike while installing one in North Carolina. For all of his work, Powers was given the 1991 President's Stewardship Award by the Nature Conservancy.

True/False

1. Ferrous metals contain either iron or elements alloyed with iron to make steel. T F

2. Manganese and lead are abundant metals. T F

3. Most ores in the U.S are extracted through subsurface mining. T F

4. The U.S. contains adequate deposits of most strategic and critical minerals. T F

5 Mineral scarcity is primarily determined by the amount of known reserves. T F

Fill in the Blank

1. Minerals are formed through geologic processes involving the cooling of _____ from the earth's core.

2. Where concentration of a mineral is high enough to make mining economically feasible, the deposit is known as a(n) _____.

3. _____ is the vegetation, soil, and rock removed during surface mining.

4. A mineral considered essential to a nation's defense is called a(n)

_____.

5. To provide a reserve of strategic and critical minerals in the event of a sudden cutoff or embargo, the U.S. _____ these minerals.

Multiple Choice

Choose the best answer.

1. Which of the following is true of U.S. mineral consumption?
   A. The U.S. consumes more iron than any other country.
   B. The U.S. consumes about 30% of total global mineral production.
   C. The U.S. consumes fewer critical mineral resources than most MDCs.
   D. None of the above is true.

2. Mineral resources which have been discovered but which **cannot yet be extracted** at a profit are known as
   A. proven resources.
   B. subeconomic resources.
   C. recoverable resources.
   D. economic resources.

3. The most environmentally benign step in the mining process is
   A. exploration.
   B. extraction.
   C. processing.
   D. All of the above are equally damaging.

4. About _____ of recyclable mineral resources in the U.S. are recycled.
   A. 60%
   B. 40%
   C. 20%
   D. 10%

5. Which of the following is a type of advanced material?
   A. superconductors
   B. composites
   C. ceramics
   D. All of the above are true.

Short Answer

1. List and briefly describe the three types of rocks.

2. List and briefly describe the different classifications of minerals.

3. Explain the difference between critical and strategic minerals.

180

4. What is the Law of the Sea?

5. What is a composite?

Thought Questions

Develop a complete answer for each of the following.

1. How are mineral deposits formed?

2. Discuss estimates of mineral deposits. Why is it unlikely that we will exhaust mineral resources?

3. Describe the steps in the mining process and discuss the environmental effects of each step.

4. Discuss the economic and environmental implications of mining deposits in Antarctica and the oceans.

5. Discuss the factors that affect mineral production and consumption.

6. Describe the conflict between mining laws and environmental conservation in the U.S.

7. How can mineral resource supplies be conserved?

Related Concepts

Describe the relationship. (There may be more than one.)

BETWEEN...	AND...
mineral distribution	tectonic activity
geology	mineral exploration
tailings	overburden
Mining Law of 1872	Mineral Leasing Act of 1920
advanced materials	conservation of mineral resources

Suggested Activities

1. Learn about ways in which you can recycle materials, and begin recycling. Encourage your friends and family to do the same. Find out what happens to the materials you recycle.

2. Write your Congressional representative and ask them to work for the repeal of the Mining Law of 1872.

3. Visit a mining site.

CHAPTER 18

Nuclear Resources

Chapter Outline

A. Prevent Overuse Through Conservation

B. Protect Human Health and the Environment

C. Preserve Living Systems

Learning Objectives

After learning the material in Chapter 18 you should be able to:

1. Define nuclear energy and describe how a nuclear fission reaction occurs.

2. Define "ionizing radiation," list its various cultural and natural sources, and describe the particles and rays emitted.

3. Describe the different applications of nuclear technology.

4. Identify four types of waste produced by a nuclear power plant.

5. Explain two types of exposure to radiation and the possible health and environmental effects.

6. Define "fusion" and list the advantages and disadvantages associated with its use as an energy source.

7. Identify the issues involved in long-term storage of nuclear waste.

8. Identify the various means by which radiation has improved human life.

9. Identify the Hanford Federal Facility, what was produced there, and the problems associated with that production.

Did You Know . . . ?

Ninety times more radiation was released from the Chernobyl accident than from the atomic explosion at Hiroshima.

Key Concepts

Read this summary of Chapter 18 and identify the important concepts discussed in the chapter.

Nuclear resources are derived from atoms, their energy, and the particles they emit. Nuclear energy is the energy released, or radiated, from an atom. Energy released from an atom is called radiation. Radiation takes two basic forms: ionizing and nonionizing.

Ionizing radiation travels in waves or as particles. The energy level of ionizing radiation is high enough to remove electrons from atoms, creating charged particles called ions. As ionizing radiation penetrates living tissue, it can destroy cells or alter their genetic structure. The effects of radiation on living organisms depend on several factors: amount of exposure, age and gender of the organisms, and type of exposure.

Nonionizing radiation can also affect atoms, but its energy level is not high enough to create ions.

Nuclear energy is released through three types of reactions: spontaneous radioactivity, fission, and fusion.

Spontaneous radioactivity occurs when unstable atoms release mass in the form of particles (particulate radiation), energy in the form of waves (electromagnetic radiation), or both.

A fission reaction occurs when an atom is split into two or more new atoms.

A fusion reaction occurs when nuclei are forced to combine. It is the opposite of a fission reaction.

Ionizing radiation affects human health as it penetrates living tissue. This penetration can destroy cells or alter their genetic structure. The effects of radiation on human beings are dependent upon the amount of exposure they receive, as well as age and gender.

Nuclear resources are used in a variety of ways, including medical applications, food preservation, power sources, for satellites, production of metal alloys, generation of electricity, and military applications.

In 1947 the government established the Atomic Energy Commission (AEC) to control the use of and disclosure of information on atomic power. When the Soviet Union detonated its first atomic bomb in 1949, the nuclear arms race between that country and the United States began.

The use of nuclear resources has been accompanied by many environmental and social problems. Among the most serious are radioactive leaks, accidents at nuclear power plants, disposal of radioactive wastes, decommissioning of old plants, and the secrecy surrounding nuclear activities.

Key Terms

nuclear resource

nuclear energy

radiation

ion

isotope

radioisotope

alpha particle

beta particle

gamma radiation

x-ray

half-life

critical mass

chain reaction

direct exposure

radioactive fallout

indirect exposure

nuclear winter

containment vessel

uranium mill tailings

low-level radioactive waste

transuranic radioactive waste

high-level radioactive waste

decommission

Environmental Success Story

After learning that the facility across the street from her home in Fernald, Ohio was a DOE uranium plant instead of the animal food factory she assumed it was, Lisa Crawford became angry. She then found out that the DOE knew about uranium levels in water that were 30 times greater than the level considered safe. She joined the Fernald Residents for Environmental Safety and Health (FRESH), and soon became the leader in the fight against the plant. Lisa and her husband Ken were the first plaintiffs in a $300 million suit against National Lead of Ohio (NLO), which operated the plant under contract with the DOE. In 1989, the lawsuit was finally settled and DOE agreed to pay $78 million damage to residents of Fernald. However, the damage payment comes from the taxpayers, because the DOE's contract with NLO left them in charge in case of problems with the plant. FRESH's activities are not done, even after this great victory; they plan on working until the whole facility is cleaned up.

True/False

1. Most of the radiation released to the environment comes from natural sources.   T   F

2. Doses of 5 rems or more per year are considered high-level exposure.   T   F

3. According to the Nuclear Regulatory Commission, the maximum safe exposure for the general public is 0.17 millirem per year.   T   F

4. The 1963 Nuclear Test Ban Treaty halted above-ground testing.   T   F

5. Nuclear power produces only about 5% of the total electricity produced in the U.S.   T   F

Fill in the Blank

1. The period it takes for half of the atoms of a radioactive material to decay into the next element is its _____.

2. Dirt and debris contaminated with radiation is called _____ .

3. The radioactive element cobalt 60 is used in the process of _____ to kill bacteria, insects, and fungi on produce.

4. Although uranium is the most commonly used fissionable material today, another radioactive element being explored for the production of energy is _____ .

5. When a nuclear power plant becomes to old to function, it is _____ by dismantling and decontaminating the reactor.

Multiple Choice

Choose the best answer.

1. Ionizing radiation
   A. travels in particles and waves.
   B. is produced by fission reactions.
   C. is capable of damaging living tissue.
   D. All of the above are true.

2. Negatively charged particles that contain more energy than electrons are
   A. alpha particles.
   B. beta particles.
   C. gamma rays.
   D. x-rays.

3. The amount of radiation absorbed per gram of tissue is expressed in units called
   A. rads.
   B. rems.
   C. sieverts.
   D. None of the above is true.

4. A problem associated with older nuclear power plants is
   A. corroded fuel rods.
   B. brittle steel pressure vessels.
   C. pressurized reactor core.
   D. All of the above are true.

5. Waste that contains human-made radioactive elements with an atomic number higher than uranium is called
   A. low-level radioactive waste.
   B. high-level radioactive waste.
   C. transuranic radioactive waste.
   D. None of the above is true.

Short Answer

1. What is a nuclear winter?

2. Where was the world's first commercial nuclear reactor built?

3. What were the stipulations of the 1968 Nuclear Non-Proliferation Treaty?

4. What is a meltdown?

5. What is PUREX?

Thought Questions

Develop a complete answer for each of the following.

1. Describe what happens in a fusion reaction. What are the barriers to producing man-made fusion reactions? Is fusion the answer to the problems caused by fission reactions?

2. Discuss the known effects of radiation on human health. Explain what is meant by low level and high level doses. What factors seem to affect susceptibility?

3. How do we use nuclear resources? What are the major risks? What are the strongest arguments for and against using nuclear resources?

4. What are the environmental effects of nuclear energy? How does it compare with other energy sources?

5. Describe the evolution of our use of nuclear resources, from the Manhattan Project up to the present day. What has been the U.S. government's role in the development of nuclear resources?

6. Explain the methods of disposing of different kinds of nuclear wastes and describe the problems associated with each.

Related Concepts

Describe the relationship. (There may be more than one.)

BETWEEN...	AND...	
fission	fusion	
indirect exposure	radioactive rain	
low-level radioactive waste	high-level radioactive waste	
Atomic Energy Commission	Department of Energy	

Did You Know . . . ?

Over 23,000 square miles of forests have been destroyed due to air pollution.

Suggested Activities

1. Find out if your home receives energy from a nuclear power plant or plants. Investigate it. How long has it been in operation? What is its safety record?

2. Do some more research on the Yucca Mountain, Nevada, site selected by the Department of Energy for storage of high-level waste. What is planned for the site? What are the barriers to its construction?

3. Test your home for radon gas.

CHAPTER 19

Toxic and Hazardous Substances

Chapter Outline

I. Describing Toxic and Hazardous Resources

    A. Physical Boundaries

        1. What Are Toxic and Hazardous Substances?

        2. What Is the Difference Between Toxic and Hazardous Substances?

        3. How Do Toxic and Hazardous Substances Enter the Environment?

    B. Biological Boundaries

        1. How Do Toxic and Hazardous Substances Affect Environmental Health?

        2. How Do Toxic and Hazardous Substances Affect Human Health?

    C. Social Boundaries

        1. Who Produces and Uses Toxic and Hazardous Substances?

        2. What Are Household Hazardous Wastes?

        3. How Do Toxic and Hazardous Substances Affect Communities?

            a. Bhopal, India

II. History of Management

    A. What Is Incineration?

    B. What Is Landfilling?

C. What Is Deep-Well Injection?

D. How Are Toxic and Hazardous Substances Treated to Reduce the Risk of Environmental Contamination?

E. What Is Waste Minimization?

    1. Reducing the Amount of Hazardous Substances Used and the Volume of Wastes Produced

    2. Reducing the Volume of Hazardous Wastes that Must Be Disposed Of

F. What Are Waste Exchanges?

G. What Legislation Affects the Management of Toxic and Hazardous Substances?

    1. Superfund

    2. Resource Conservation and Recovery Act

        a. Regulating Hazardous Wastes

        b. Cradle to Grave Management of Hazardous Wastes

    3. Toxic Substances Control Act

III. Future Management of Toxic and Hazardous Substances

A. Prevent Overuse of Resources

B. Protect Human Health and Environment

C. Preserve Living Systems

Learning Objectives

After learning the material in Chapter 19 you should be able to:

1. Explain the difference between toxic substances and hazardous substances.

2. List and describe the potential effects on human health resulting from exposure to hazardous and toxic substances.

3. Describe what happened at Love Canal, New York, and its importance in the management of hazardous waste.

4. Explain the social dimensions and consequences of hazardous waste production and disposal.

5. Describe at least three different methods of disposing of hazardous waste.

6. Identify the major pieces of legislation which affect the management of hazardous and toxic wastes in the United States.

7. Define the concept of waste minimization and explain why it has become so important.

8. Identify Clean Sites, Inc., and describe the importance of the work this organization has done.

Did You Know . . . ?

The Pentagon produces twice as much hazardous waste as the top three industrial waste producers.

Key Concepts

Read this summary of Chapter 19 and identify the important concepts discussed in the chapter.

Toxic and hazardous substances are chemicals that can adversely affect human health and the environment. This broad definition can include elements (ex. lead), compounds (ex. polychlorinated biphenyls, or PCBs), and the products of infectious agents like bacteria and protozoans.

Many toxic and hazardous substances occur naturally in the earth's crust and biota; others are manufactured by industrial processes.

Although the terms "toxic" and "hazardous" are often used interchangeably, they are not synonymous. The term "toxic" implies the potential to cause injury to living organisms. Almost any substance can be toxic under the right conditions, if the concentration is high enough or if an organism is exposed to the substance for long enough. The term "hazardous" implies that there is some chance that the organism will be exposed to a substance and that that exposure will result in harm. Substances can be considered hazardous only when a possibility exists that plants and animals will be exposed to them.

The 1976 passage of the Resource Conservation and Recovery Act (RCRA) provided the EPA with a statutory framework for defining hazardous waste. Accordingly, a hazardous waste is defined as any solid, liquid, or gaseous waste which, due to its quantity, concentration, or physical chemical, of infectious characteristics, may cause or significantly contribute to an increase in mortality or serious illness; or pose a substantial present or potential hazard to human health or the environment when improperly stored, transported, disposed of, or recycled.

Toxic and hazardous substances are released into the environment as by-products, as end products, or through the use and disposal of manufactured products. They are of serious concern because of their potential and suspected adverse effects on ecosystems and living organisms, including humans.

Toxic and hazardous substances affect human health in a variety of ways. Acute toxicity is the occurrence of serious symptoms immediately after a single exposure to a substance. Chronic toxicity is the delayed appearance of symptoms until a substance accumulates to a threshold level in the body after repeated exposures to the substance. There are also a number of general ways in which hazardous and toxic substances affect long-term human health. Carcinogenic substances can cause cancer in humans and animals. Infectious substances contain disease-causing organisms. Teratogenic substances affect the unborn fetus; they may cause birth defects or spontaneous abortions or otherwise damage the fetus. Mutagenic substances cause genetic changes or mutations, which then appear in future generations.

Toxic chemicals can be found in garages and kitchen sinks all across America. They are considered to be household hazardous items if there are hazards involved in their use or disposal. Congress has exempted household hazardous wastes from RCRA regulations. Thus, these toxins can be legally hauled off to the local municipal landfill or solid waste incinerator for disposal.

Wastes are disposed of by burning them, burying them, or pumping them underground. Prior to disposal, most hazardous and toxic materials can be treated to reduce their hazardous nature. Methods of treatment can be classified as either chemical, physical, or biological.

Waste minimization is an umbrella term that refers to a variety of strategies to reduce the amount of toxic and hazardous substances used and the volume of hazardous waste that must be disposed of. Waste minimization strategies are based on the premise that toxic and hazardous substances are resources that can and should be managed in environmentally sound ways. While they cannot eliminate all hazardous wastes, these strategies can enable business, industry, and households to mimic natural systems, thereby becoming less wasteful and more efficient.

Toxic and hazardous substances are managed according to the provisions of three major laws: the Comprehensive Environmental Response, Compensation, and Liability Act (CERCLA), called Superfund; the Resource Conservation and Recovery Act (RCRA); and the Toxic Substances Control Act (TSCA).

Key Terms

acute toxicity

bioremediation

carcinogenic

chemical sensitizer

chronic toxicity

component separation process

hazardous

hazardous waste

infectious

leachate

multiple chemical sensitivity (MCS)

mutagenic

phase separation process

sanitary landfill

secure landfill

solidification

source segregation

still bottoms

teratogenic

toxic

waste minimization

Environmental Success Story

After it was determined that her baby sister had died because her mother had drunk contaminated water, Kory Johnson took a stand against pollution. The twelve-year-old from Phoenix, Arizona founded a group called Children for a Safe Environment. One of their greatest accomplishments was leading a protest against a hazardous waste incinerator that planned to burn 70% of its waste from suppliers outside the state. Although the state had made a deal with the company, the governor called off the deal on May 4, 1991 because of the huge amount of public pressure against the incinerator. As a result of her work for the environment, Kory received John Denver's Windstar Environmental Youth Award.

True/False

1. The U.S. produces 270 million tons of hazardous waste each year. T F

2. All known carcinogens are also mutagens. T F

3. Texas produces more toxic substances than any other state. T F

4. Deep-well injection of hazardous wastes is the final solution to the disposal of nonrecyclable hazardous liquids. T F

5. The Resource Conservation and Recovery Act of 1976 regulates the disposal of hazardous household wastes. T F

Fill in the Blank

1. A substance which causes birth defects is known as a _____ substance.

2. Worldwide, most hazardous wastes are generated and disposed of by the _____ , _____ , and _____ industries.

3. The process of entombing hazardous wastes into concrete blocks is called _____ .

4. _____ are engineered to prevent the escape of leachate.

5. The Comprehensive, Environmental Response, Compensation, and Liability Act is better known as _____ .

Multiple Choice

Choose the best answer.

1. Lead poisoning is an example of
   A. acute toxicity
   B. chronic toxicity
   C. mutagenic effect
   D. None of the above is true.

2. All of the following are drawbacks of incinerating hazardous substances except
   A. a large amount of bottom ash is generated
   B. hazardous combustion products may form
   C. particulate metals are not destroyed
   D. PCBs are not destroyed

3. All of the following are examples of physical treatment of hazardous waste except
   A. centrifugation
   B. component separation
   C. landfarming
   D. solidification

4. The legislation that regulates the production, distribution, and use of toxic substances is the
   A. RCRA
   B. CERCLA
   C. TSCA
   D. EPA

5. _____is the delayed appearance of symptoms until a substance accumulates to a threshold level in the body after repeated exposures to the substance.
   A. Acute toxicity
   B. Chronic toxicity
   C. Abrupt toxicity
   D. Absolute toxicity

Short Answer

1. Explain the difference between a toxic substance and a hazardous substance.

2. What is MCS?

3. What techniques are used in secure landfills to prevent rainwater from percolating through the wastes?

4. What are waste exchanges?

5. What are the four hazardous waste characteristics defined by RCRA?

Thought Questions

Develop a complete answer for each of the following.

1. Why are the poor often at the greatest risk of exposure to toxic substances? Discuss the social issues surrounding this phenomenon.

2. Compare incineration, landfilling, and deep-well injection as methods of disposing of hazardous and toxic wastes. What are the major strengths and weaknesses of each method?

3. How does bioremediation differ from the chemical and physical methods of treating hazardous wastes?

4. Why has waste minimization become so important? Discuss strategies for reducing wastes.

5. Explain how the three major pieces of legislation are used to manage toxic substances from production to disposal. How effective is this legislation at protecting both humans and the environment from the effects of toxic substances?

Related Concepts

Describe the relationship. (There may be more than one.)

BETWEEN...	AND...
acute toxicity	chronic toxicity
bottom ash	still bottoms
TSCA	RCRA
CERCLA	Superfund
Superfund	Clean Sites, Inc.

Did You Know . . . ?

Eighty percent of the chemicals sprayed on crops are sprayed for beautification.

Suggested Activities

1. Start a local household hazardous materials collection program. (See "What You Can Do to Minimize Dangers of Toxic and Hazardous Substances.")

2. Research the history of a Superfund National Priority List site. Discover how it is being cleaned up.

3. Perform a hazardous and toxic substances audit of your home. What substances do you keep around that are potentially harmful to you or the environment? Find out how they should be disposed of.

4. Begin using biodegradable and environmentally friendly substances as replacements for hazardous ones.

CHAPTER 20

Unrealized Resources: Waste Minimization and Resource Recovery

Chapter Outline

I.   Describing Unrealized Resources

    A. Physical Boundaries

        1. What Is Solid Waste?

        2. What Solid Wastes Can Be Recovered from the Solid Waste Stream?

            a. Aluminum

            b. Paper

            c. Cardboard

            d. Glass

            e. Plastics

            f. Iron and Steel

            g. Tires

            h. Used Oil

            i. White Goods

            j. Food and Yard Wastes

B. Biological Boundaries

    1. How Do Living Systems Manage Waste Products?

    2. How Can Humans Mimic the Action of Living Systems?

C. Social Boundaries

    1. How Do Waste Production and Management Vary Worldwide?

    2. What Misconceptions Are Associated with Solid Waste Disposal?

II. History of Management of Unrealized Resources

  A. What Is Ocean Dumping?

  B. What Is Landfilling?

    1. How Landfills Operate

    2. Environmental, Economic, and Social Problems Associated with Landfills

      a. Closing of Existing Landfills

      b. Lack of Appropriate Sites for New Landfills

      c. Rising Economic Costs

      d. Community Opposition to the Siting of New Landfills

      e. Leachate Contamination

  C. What Is Incineration?

    1. Environmental and Economic Problems Associated with Incineration

    2. What Is Waste Minimization?

    3. What Is Resource Recovery?

      a. Recycling

Learning Objectives

After learning the material in Chapter 20 you should be able to:

1. Describe how contemporary society differs from previous cultures in terms of solid waste.

2. Explain what is meant by unrealized resources and give some examples of these resources.

3. Differentiate between municipal and industrial solid wastes, and define the solid waste stream.

4. Describe the recycling capabilities of aluminum, paper, glass, plastic, iron/steel, scrap tires, "white goods," and organic matter.

5. Explain how living systems manage waste products, and describe how humans can mimic the action of living systems.

6. Describe how the generation and management of solid wastes vary worldwide.

7. Identify the major waste disposal methods in the United States and describe each.

8. Identify the myths associated with landfill disposal.

9. Define waste minimization and resource recovery and explain why they are preferable to waste disposal.

10. Identify the New Alchemy Institute and the importance of its research.

Did You Know . . . ?

Texas has the most landfills in the United States.

Key Concepts

Read this summary of Chapter 20 and identify the important concepts discussed in the chapter.

A solid waste is any material that is rejected or discarded as being spent, useless, worthless, or in excess. The solid waste stream is the collective and continual production of all refuse. The two largest sources of solid wastes are agriculture and mining. Municipal solid waste (MSW) is refuse generated by households, businesses, and institutions. Solid wastes, like hazardous wastes, are misplaced or unrealized resources.

Natural systems are cyclic; in contrast, human systems tend to be linear. As the law of the conservation of matter indicates, materials can be neither created nor destroyed. The most promising solution to the solid waste problem is to reuse and recycle wastes as much as possible. Materials that can be recovered from the solid waste stream include: aluminum, paper, cardboard, glass, plastics, iron and steel, tires, used oil, white goods (old appliances), and food/yard wastes.

For materials that cannot be recycled, the solution is to reduce consumption or to substitute nonhazardous alternatives for them.

Both the consumption of goods and the management of waste products vary from country to country. The waste stream of less-developed countries is typically much smaller than that of more-developed countries.

Historically, most civilizations have managed their refuse in one of four ways: dumping it, burning it, converting it into something that can be used again, or reducing the amount of wastes produced.

Landfills are created by dumping refuse, then burying it beneath layers of earth and additional garbage. The Resource Conservation and Recovery Act established classifications for various types of landfills. Secure landfills, which have a heavy plastic liner and a clay cap, are designed to contain hazardous wastes. Sanitary landfills, lined with thick layers of clay or plastic, are built to receive nonhazardous residential, commercial, and industrial wastes.

The environmental, economic, and social problems associated with landfills include: closing existing landfills, rising economic costs, lack of appropriate sites for new landfills, community opposition to siting new landfills, and the possibility of leachate contamination.

Incineration offers some attractive alternatives to landfilling: it can reduce the volume of waste by 80 to 90 percent, and waste-to-energy incinerators burn garbage to produce heat. However, air pollution and the need to landfill the remaining ash are two of the environmental problems that result.

Waste minimization, or source reduction, includes minimizing the volume of products, minimizing packaging, extending the useful life of products, and minimizing the amount of toxic substances in products. As consumers, we can all practice waste minimization via precycling. Precycling is a conscious effort to purchase merchandise that has a minimal adverse effect on the environment.

Resource recovery is an umbrella term that refers to the taking of useful materials or energy out of the waste stream before ultimate disposal. Recycling (the collection, processing, and marketing of waste material in new products) and composting (converting organic wastes to useful soil material) are two means of resource recovery.

Interest in waste minimization and resource recovery is increasing as communities seek new ways of managing their growing waste stream.

Green marketing -- the practice of promoting products based on the claims that they help or are benign to the environment -- is more prevalent as American consumers are becoming more aware of environmental issues.

Key Terms

aerobic decomposition

anaerobic decomposition

co-composting

co-mingled recycling

curbside collection

garbage

green marketing

integrated solid waste system

mass burn incinerator

municipal solid waste (MSW)

precycling

recycling

refuse

refuse-derived fuel incinerator

resource recovery

sanitary landfills

secondary materials

secure landfills

solid waste

solid waste stream

source reduction

source separation

tipping fee

trash

unrealized resource

waste minimization

waste-to-energy incinerator

Environmental Success Story

Earthworm Inc., a nonprofit company that operates in the Boston area, has been recycling wastepaper for 20 years and has become self-sufficient, unlike most other recyclers, who operate with government aid. Their mission is to advocate recycling and to serve those companies that the private sector does not find it profitable to do business with. By collecting during the day, unlike most recyclers who collect at night to avoid parking tickets, Earthworm employees develop relationships with the people they serve. Their hope is to change people's attitudes toward saving instead of throwing away.

True/False

1.   More than 50% of all aluminum cans in the U.S. are recycled.   T   F

2.   Most of the decomposition in a landfill is aerobic.   T   F

3.   All plastics are nonbiodegradable.   T   F

4.   With 5% of the world's population, the United States generates   T   F
     about 20% of the world's waste.

5.   The lifespan of a typical landfill is about 10 years.   T   F

Fill in the Blank

1. The largest single component by volume of U.S. landfills is .

2. Crushed recycled glass, used to make new glass, is called   .

3. A(n) _____ is charged by landfills for disposal of wastes.

4. Refuse may be compacted into pellets for use in a(n)   .

5. The effort of consumers to purchase merchandise that has a minimal adverse effect on the environment is called _____ .

Multiple Choice

Choose the best answer.

1. About _____ % of the U.S. solid waste stream is municipal solid waste.
A. 3
B. 9
C. 18
D. 41

2. About 10% of the solid waste stream is generated by_____activities.
A. residential
B. industrial
C. agricultural
D. mining

3. Which of the following is recycled for use in automobiles and as home insulation?
A. aluminum
B. glass
C. newsprint
D. plastic

4. Plastics account for about _____% of the average landfill's contents by volume.
A. 5
B. 12
C. 20
D. 31

5. ___ landfills are designed to receive nonhazardous residential, commercial, and industrial wastes.

   A. Safety
   B. Secure
   C. Sanitary
   D. Sealed

Short Answer

1. What are the two largest sources of solid waste in the U.S.?

2. What are the three types of plastics that are most commonly recycled?

3. Name and describe the function of the three types of soil-dwelling bacteria that are responsible for most of the decomposition that occurs in landfills.

4. What is a "biodegradable plastic"?

5. What is green marketing?

Thought Questions

Develop a complete answer for each of the following.

1. Which elements of the municipal solid waste stream are being recycled in the U.S.? Which are not? Discuss the use of the recycled materials.

2. Compare natural and human systems for handling wastes.

3. Discuss how waste production and management vary worldwide.

4. Discuss the environmental, economic, and social problems associated with landfills.

5. Compare landfilling, ocean dumping, and incineration as methods of disposing of waste.

6. Discuss the economics of recycling.

Related Concepts

Describe the relationship. (There may be more than one.)

BETWEEN...	AND...
glasphalt	fiberglass
white goods	hazardous waste
landfill	composting
plastics	ocean dumping
waste minimization	resource recovery

> **Did You Know . . . ?**
>
> The energy saved by recycling one aluminum can could operate a TV for three hours. The energy saved by recycling a glass bottle could light a 60 watt bulb for four hours.

Suggested Activities

1. By recycling, reuse, and source reduction of materials, how much can you reduce the amount of garbage you throw away each week? Start your own integrated waste management program. Keep a record of the types of materials, and how you handle them. If you already do some of these things, see if you can increase the amount you recover or reduce.

2. Where does the trash generated in your community go? Investigate, and report your findings.

3. Reduce the amount of waste you produce by precycling. (See "What You Can Do: To Precycle.")

4. Support deposit legislation. Urge your state representatives to pass a statewide bottle bill, and tell your member of Congress you support deposit legislation worldwide.

UNIT SIX

AN ENVIRONMENTAL HERITAGE

CHAPTER 21

The Public Lands

Chapter Outline

I. Describing the Public Lands Resource

    A. Biological Boundaries

        1. What Are the Federal Public Lands?

            a. National Park System

            b. National Wildlife Refuge System

            c. National Forest System

            d. National Resource Lands

        2. Why Are the Public Lands Biologically Significant?

    B. Physical Boundaries

    C. Social Boundaries

II. History of Management of the Public Lands

    A. How Did the System of Federal Lands Develop?

    B. How Did the National Park System Develop?

    C. What Environmental Problems Face the National Park System?

        1. Internal Threats to the National Park System

            a. Overuse

            b. Insufficient Funding and Park Operations

            c. Threats to Wildlife

d. Concessions System

e. Energy and Minerals Development

2. External Threats to the National Park System

a. Atmospheric Pollution

b. Activities on Adjacent Lands

D. How Did the National Wildlife Refuge System Develop?

E. What Environmental Problems Face the National Wildlife Refuge System?

1. Internal Threats to the National Wildlife Refuge System

a. Management Structure

b. Secondary Uses

2. External Threats to the National Wildlife Refuge System

a. Activities on Adjacent Lands

b. Political Pressures

F. How Did the National Forest System Develop?

G. What Environmental Problems Face the National Forest System?

1. Emphasis on Logging Over Other Uses

2. Clear-cutting

3. Below-Cost Timber Sales

4. Wilderness Designation -- Commercial Activities Can Make Land Ineligible for this Protection

H. How Did the Network of National Resource Lands Develop?

I. What Environmental Problems Face the National Resource Lands?

1. Illegal Harvesting and Disruptive Recreational Use

2. Commercial Exploitation

3. Wilderness Designation -- Land Needs This Designation to Preserve Its Ecological Integrity, Beauty, and Unique Character

J. What Initiatives Are Being Taken to Protect the Federal Lands?

1. National Park System

2. National Wildlife Refuge System

3. National Forest System

4. National Resource Lands

III. Future Management of the Public Lands

A. Prevent Overuse Through Conservation

B. Protect Human Health and the Environment

C. Preserve Living Systems

Learning Objectives

After learning the material in Chapter 21 you should be able to:

1. Trace the history of the public land resource in the United States, from the federal government's encouraging settlement to its preservation of ecosystems.

2. Identify the history, size, management goals, and environmental problems associated with the following: National Park System, National Wildlife Refuge System, National Forest System, and the National Resource Lands.

3. Describe the conflicts associated with "commercial versus recreational," and "consumptive versus non-consumptive" uses of our national public lands.

4. List and explain the important pieces of legislation which have influenced our current methods of managing the public land resource, including the Multiple-Use, Sustained Yield Act, the Organic Act, the Forest Reserve Act, and the Federal Land Policy and Management Act.

5. Identify the recent federal initiatives designed to protect public lands, including the President's Commission on Americans Outdoors and the National Park System Protection and Resource Act.

6. Identify the problems associated with accommodating large crowds at National Parks, and how officials at Yosemite National Park decided to handle this dilemma.

Did You Know . . . ?

A pair of Northern spotted owls needs 5,000 acres of old growth forest to survive.

Key Concepts

Read this summary of Chapter 21 and identify the important concepts discussed in the chapter.

The federal lands, or public domain, include approximately 700 million acres of forest, desert, grassland, wetland, and other lands. They are managed by numerous federal agencies, chiefly the Park Service (Department of Interior), Fish and Wildlife Service (Department of Interior), Forest Service (Department of Agriculture), and Bureau of Land Management (Department of Interior).

The National Park System encompasses 343 diverse units totaling almost 80 million acres. The Park Service strives to manage the parks in order to conserve their scenery, natural and historic objects, and wildlife, and to provide for the enjoyment and use of the same by the public. Major threats to the Park System are crowding and overuse, insufficient funding and park operations, diminishing habitat, elimination of predators, poaching, commercial recreational opportunities, energy and minerals development, atmospheric pollution, and activities conducted on adjacent lands.

The National Wildlife Refuge System (NWRS) is a network of 456 units totaling about 91 million acres of land and water in 49 states and 5 territories. They provide habitat and haven for wildlife. Major threats to the National Wildlife Refuges are the internal management structure of the USFWS, which is plagued by too many competing responsibilities, harmful or incompatible secondary uses on many refuges, activities on adjacent lands, and political pressures.

The National Forest System encompasses approximately 191 million acres in 44 states, Puerto Rico and the Virgin Islands. The nation's forests and grasslands are multiple use lands -- they accommodate both commercial and recreational uses as well as wilderness habitat. Major threats to the National Forests are an emphasis on logging over other uses, clearcutting, below cost timber sales, and lack of wilderness designation/protection.

Multiple use is also the philosophy that governs the National Resource Lands or BLM lands. Found chiefly in the arid and semi-arid western states and Alaska, BLM lands equal approximately 300 million acres, almost half of all federal land. Even though they form the largest block of federal lands, BLM lands receive relatively few visitors. Major threats to the National Resource Lands include looting, poaching, and illegal harvesting, commercial exploitation (especially grazing), and lack of wilderness designation.

The biological significance of the federal lands has to do with the variety of ecosystems they contain, the biological diversity they harbor, and the ecosystem services they perform. The physical boundaries of the federal lands pertains to their mineral wealth; these areas contain one-quarter of the nation's coal, four-fifths of its huge oil-shale deposits, one-half of its uranium deposits and naturally occurring steam and hotwater pools, one-half of its estimated oil and gas reserves, and significant reserves of strategic minerals.

The social significance of the federal lands has to do with how they are used. Commercial consumptive uses include logging, mining, and oil development. Nonconsumptive recreational uses include scientific study, wilderness travel, hiking, birdwatching, and canoeing. It is important to realize that non-consumptive uses such as hiking or trailbiking can degrade an area if there are many users or if the users are not careful about the way in which they use the land.

When we look at the history of the federal lands, we see that it is largely one of land disposal to private interests. In the early nineteenth century, land disposal was seen as a way of encouraging western expansion and settlement and thus securing the nation's frontier. As early as 1832, the government began to set aside land units for special purposes. It was not until a hundred years later, however, in the mid 1930s, that all public lands in the lower 48 states were withdrawn from homesteading. That act marked the beginning of protection for the remaining public domain.

In recent years, the public lands have been the subject of intense public scrutiny. Many people are concerned with problems such as overcrowding, insufficient funding, lack of wilderness designation and protection, and others. Legislation has been proposed to protect and improve the management of the National Parks and Refuges. Public input has led to more balanced management plans for several of the nation's forests. Plans have also been proposed to better manage BLM lands. Chief among these is a proposal to phase out controversial below-market grazing fees.

Key Terms

below-cost timber sales

clear-cutting

consumptive use

multiple use

nonconsumptive use

public domain

utilitarianism

Environmental Success Story

While working at a nursery over 50 years ago, Frank H. Lockyear saw that boxes of cedar seedlings were lined up to go into a burn pile. He was able to acquire the unwanted trees and plant them, and he has been planting trees ever since. Lockyear, now in his seventies, has been responsible for planting over one million trees. He founded Retree International in 1980 with three goals: to plant trees, to educate the public on the importance of planting trees, and to assist in forestry research.

True/False

1. Nonconsumptive uses are not considered a threat to the National Parks.　　T　　F

2. The public lands account for approximately one-third of the total area of the U.S.　　T　　F

3. Mining is permitted in National Forests.   T   F

4. BLM lands are located only in Alaska and the western states.   T   F

5. The Department of the Interior and the Department of   T   F
   Agriculture share the responsibility for all public lands.

Fill in the Blank

1. The BLM lands are officially known as _ _ _ _ _ _ _ _ _ _ _ _ _ _ _ .

2. Bird-watching and photography are examples of _ _ _ _ _ _ _ _ _ .

3. President Theodore Roosevelt broadened the intent of the _ _ _ _ _ _ _ _ Act to
   preserve significant natural areas.

4. The commission formed in the 1980s to determine what needs were unmet by
   the present system of public lands was called the _ _ _ _ _ _ _ _ .

5. Historically, the _ _ _ _ _ _ _ _ _ _ _ _ _ _ _ _ _ were set aside to protect places of
   spectacular scenery or natural grandeur.

Multiple Choice

Choose the best answer.

1. Which has the largest land area?
   A. National Park System
   B. National Wildlife Refuge System
   C. National Forest System
   D. National Resource Lands

2. The National Forest System is managed by the
   A. National Park Service.
   B. U.S. Fish and Wildlife Service.
   C. Department of Agriculture.
   D. Department of the Interior.

3. Which agency manages the National Wildlife Refuge System?
   A. National Park Service
   B. U.S. Fish and Wildlife Service
   C. Department of Agriculture
   D. None of the above is true.

4. The purpose of the National Forest System is to
   A. provide habitat for wildlife.
   B. manage for sustained multiple use.
   C. preserve the natural scenery and provide for use by the public.
   D. None of the above is true.

5. Historically, which practice governed the management of the public domain?
   A. multiple use
   B. disposal to private interests
   C. protectionism
   D. isolationism

Short Answer

1. What is the Bureau of Reclamation?

2. What is a split estate?

3. What is a duck stamp?

4. List the five land uses the National Forest Service is mandated to balance.

5. Name the legislation that formed the National Park Service.

Thought Questions

Develop a complete answer for each of the following.

1. Explain the biological significance of the public lands.

2. Discuss the conflicts between commercial and recreational, consumptive and nonconsumptive uses of the federal lands.

3. Describe the major threats to the National Parks.

4. How does the structure of the Fish and Wildlife Service threaten the National Wildlife Refuge System?

5. How does the concept of utilitarianism influence the management of National Resource Lands and National Forests? Why would the managing agencies sell grazing rights and timber at below cost?

6. Discuss the effects of having the four types of federal lands managed by different agencies. How do conflicting interests strive to determine land use policy?

7. Explain the reasons behind clear-cutting and describe the impact on the environment.

Related Concepts

Describe the relationship. (There may be more than one.)

BETWEEN...	AND...
clear-cutting	flashflooding
fire management policy in Yellowstone National Park	lodgepole pine
commercial use	National Resource Lands
concessions	National Parks
chaining	juniper pine

> **Did You Know ... ?**
>
> American Samoa (76 square miles) is the most pristine United States tropical rainforest. It supports five distinct types of rainforest: coastal, lowland, mountain, ridge, and cloud.

Suggested Activities

1. Pick a public land area that interests you and get to know its natural and cultural history.

2. Join a conservation organization to support its efforts to protect public lands.

3. Visit a national park, forest, refuge or BLM land. Practice low-impact camping and hiking.

4. Let your elected officials know where you stand on issues pertaining to public lands.

CHAPTER 22

Wilderness

Chapter Outline

I. Describing the Wilderness Resource

    A. Biological Boundaries

        1. What Is Wilderness?

        2. How Can Wilderness Areas Preserve Biological Diversity?

    B. Physical Boundaries

    C. Social Boundaries

        1. Why Is It Important to Preserve Wilderness?

            a. Personal Benefits

            b. Economics

            c. Ecological Benefits

            d. Cultural Heritage

II. History of Management of Wilderness

    A. How Did the Wilderness Preservation Movement Develop?

    B. How Were Wilderness Areas Managed Prior to the Wilderness Preservation Act?

    C. How Was the Wilderness Act of 1964 Enacted?

    D. How Is An Area Designated as Wilderness?

    E. How Did the Wilderness Act Affect the Preservation and Management of the Federal Lands?

F. What Is RARE?

G. What Is the Federal Land Policy and Management Act?

H. How Are Wilderness Areas Currently Managed?

I. What Environmental Problems Face Wilderness Areas?

J. What Initiatives Are Being Undertaken to Preserve Wilderness Areas?

III. Future Management of Wilderness

A. Prevent Overuse Through Conservation

B. Protect Human Health and the Environment

C. Preserve Living Systems

Learning Objectives

After learning the material in Chapter 22 you should be able to:

1. Define "wilderness" according to the Wilderness Preservation Act and describe why it is impossible to scientifically define that term.

2. Identify the difference between genetic and ecosystem diversity and detail why each is vital.

3. List and explain the social benefits of wilderness preservation.

4. Detail the key components of Robert Marshall's "Magna Carta of Wilderness."

5. Identify the Wilderness Act of 1964, the steps involved in recommending areas for protection, and the subsequent management objectives.

6. Define the reasons why no wilderness regions were designated from 1964-1973, and how the Wilderness Act of 1973 attempted to rectify that situation.

7. Define "de facto" wilderness regions, and explain why they are considered to be threatened.

8. Describe the various reasons why the Memorandum of Understanding (MOU) is such an important agreement.

9. Trace the history of growth of The Boundary Waters Canoe Area Wilderness Region and identify the environmental concerns which continue to threaten this resource today.

Did You Know . . . ?

Thirty percent of America and Africa is wilderness.

Key Concepts

Read this summary of Chapter 22 and identify the important concepts discussed in the chapter.

A wilderness ecosystem is one in which both the biota and abiota are minimally disturbed by humans. Not surprisingly then, wilderness areas serve as reservoirs of biological diversity, or biodiversity. The single best hope to preserve maximum biodiversity is to preserve habitats (ecosystems) as wilderness. The United States' National Wilderness Preservation System, a network of some 445 units covering over 89 million acres, protects just 81 of the country's 233 distinct ecosystem types. Many ecosystems, and their resident biota, remain unprotected.

Those who argue in favor of protecting wilderness point to the personal (mental and physical well-being), economic, and ecological benefits (ecosystem services) it provides, and to the fact that it is an integral part of our nation's cultural heritage. Opponents to wilderness preservation argue that it "locks up" valuable resources which could be used for economic development and that it benefits only a minority of recreational users.

Fifty years ago, the idea of protecting and preserving wilderness was virtually unheard of. After all, for centuries, humans had feared "wild" lands. (Interestingly, the root word for wilderness is the same as the root word for bewildered -- to be confused.) In fact, since the advent of the European conquest of North America, settlers had sought to "tame" the wilderness and transform the landscape into the pastoral vistas they had left behind in Europe. A few lone voices -- Henry David Thoreau and John Muir, primarily -- sung the praises of wild lands and warned of the threat posed by unchecked development, but most people did not heed their warnings. By the early 1930s, others were sounding the alarm. Aldo Leopold, Arthur Carhart, Robert Marshall, Benton MacKaye, and Robert Sterling Yard were some of the earliest proponents of a national system of protected wilderness areas. Unfortunately, with the building boom that followed World War II, economic uses of land were emphasized over recreation and wilderness preservation. A long struggle ensued which pitted wilderness preservationists against developers and other economic forces. Finally, in 1964, the Wilderness Preservation Act was passed to counteract the emphasis on development and economic uses of the land. The Act represented the culmination of years of effort by many people, notably Howard Zahniser, who authored the legislation but did not live to see it enacted. The Wilderness Preservation Act designated 9 million acres of federal land as protected wilderness. Though the Forest Service developed regulations for the protection and management of areas already classified as wilderness, it did not recommend any additions to the system between 1964 and 1973. To correct this situation, Congress passed the Wilderness Act of 1973. By the late 1980s, the wilderness system had grown tenfold to some 89 million acres.

Only lands included in the National Wilderness Preservation System are officially managed as protected wilderness. Both officially designated areas and de facto wilderness areas face numerous threats to their ecological integrity. Among the threats to de facto wilderness are the vagaries of the designation process itself, chaining, overgrazing, and the lack of federal water rights. Threats to designated areas include increased crowds, litter, vandalism (especially at archeological sites), damaged vegetation, water pollution, and soil erosion from heavily used trails and campsites.

Key Terms

chaining

de facto wilderness

wilderness ecosystem

Environmental Success Story

After nearly two years of collection, the Liquor Distribution Branch and brewers in British Columbia have received over 12,000 pounds of plastic Hi-cones (used to secure 6-packs of beer and soft drinks) to be recycled. Most likely because of the publicized danger that these contraptions pose to wildlife, people contributed the Hi-cones without a deposit or refund involved. These used plastic yokes go to a company that recycles them into new Hi-cones.

True/False

1. The National Wilderness Preservation System represents at   T   F
   least one of each type of ecosystem found in the U.S.

2. Most designated wilderness areas are found within National T   F
   Parks.

3. Most protected wildernesses are high alpine or tundra   T   F
   ecosystems.

4. Mining or grazing is not allowed in any wilderness area.   T   F

5. The National Park Service opposed the Wilderness Act of   T   F
   1964.

Fill in the Blank

1. The key legislation which protects wilderness areas is the _ _ _ _ _ _ _ _ .

2. In 1935, Robert Marshall and other preservationists formed the   to advocate for
   wilderness preservation.

3. An area being considered for inclusion in the National Wilderness Preservation
   System is known as a(n) _ _ _ _ _ _ _ _ _ _ _ _ .

4. Wild lands that are undesignated and unprotected are called _ _ _ _ _ _ _ _ .

5. The _ is a 1990 agreement between the Bureau of
   Land Management and the Nature Conservancy.

Multiple Choice

Choose the best answer.

1. How many ecosystem types are represented in the National Wilderness Preservation System?
   A. 50
   B. 80
   C. 100
   D. 200

2. As defined by the 1964 Wilderness Preservation Act, the most important characteristic of wilderness is
   A. biological diversity.
   B. biotic and abiotic components.
   C. minimal disturbance by humans.
   D. far removed from civilization.

3. Under the Wilderness Act, who has the responsibility for designating wilderness areas?
   A. Congress
   B. National Park Service
   C. National Forest Service
   D. All of the above are true.

4. The biggest threat to undesignated wilderness areas is
   A. logging.
   B. mining.
   C. being left out of the wilderness system.
   D. chaining.

5. The fight over which national treasure led to the development of the Wilderness Preservation Act of 1964?
   A. Yellowstone
   B. Yosemite
   C. Boundary Waters Canoe Area
   D. Dinosaur National Monument

Short Answer

1. What, according to early preservationist Robert Marshall, are the most important attributes of a wilderness area?

2. Who was Howard Zahniser?

3. List three of the five objectives of wilderness management under the 1964 Wilderness Act.

4. What was RARE?

5. What are the ecological benefits of wilderness preservation?

Thought Questions

Develop a complete answer for each of the following.

1. Discuss the arguments against wilderness designation and the corresponding defense made by conservationists.

2. Discuss the value of wilderness, and explain the nature of the arguments for preserving wilderness.

3. How did the wilderness preservation movement develop in the 1920s and 1930s? What were the major obstacles faced by early preservationists?

4. How are wilderness areas managed?

5. Describe the environmental problems currently facing designated wilderness areas, and explain what is being done to protect them.

Related Concepts

Describe the relationship.   (There may be more than one.)

BETWEEN...	AND...
Arthur Carhart	Aldo Leopold
utilitarianism	wilderness preservation
Forest Service	Wilderness Act of 1973
1976 Federal Land Policy and Management Act	1964 Wilderness Act
Bureau of Land Management	wilderness designation

> **Did You Know . . . ?**
>
> Every day, two million trees are cut down in America.

Suggested Activities

1. Choose one of the members of the wilderness preservation movement mentioned in this chapter, and find out more about them and what they did in the fight to preserve wilderness.

2. Visit a wilderness area. Document your experience.

3. Locate a wilderness area on a map. Research it to discover its unique qualities.

CHAPTER 23

Biological Resources

Chapter Outline

I. Describing Biological Resources

    A. Biological Boundaries

        1. What Are Biological Resources?

        2. What Is the Relationship Between Extinction and Biological Diversity?

    B. Physical Boundaries

        1. Where Are Species Located?

    C. Social Boundaries

        1. How Do Beliefs and Attitudes Affect the Management of Biological Resources?

        2. How Do Human Activities Affect the Management of Biological Resources?

            a. Habitat Degradation and Destruction

            b. Overharvesting and Illegal Trade

            c. Selective Breeding

        3. Why Should We Preserve Biological Resources and Biological Diversity?

            a. Ecosystem Services

            b. Benefits to Agriculture, Medicine, and Industry

            c. Esthetics

d. Ethical Considerations

e. Evolutionary Potential

II. History of Management of Biological Resources

    A. How Have Biological Resources Been Managed Historically?

    B. How Are Biological Resources Currently Managed?

        1. Off-Site Management of Plants

        2. Off-Site Management of Animals

        3. Off-Site Management of Plants and Animals

            a. Biosphere Reserves

            b. Private Efforts in the United States

        4. Pros and Cons of On-Site and Off-Site Preservation

        5. What Legislation Governs the Management of Wild Species in the United States?

        6. What Legislation Governs the Management of Wild Species Internationally?

III. Future Management of Biological Resources

    A. Prevent Overuse Through Conservation

    B. Protect Human and Environmental Health

    C. Preserve Living Systems

Learning Objectives

After learning the material in Chapter 23 you should be able to:

1. Define biological resources, and identify its two types.

2. Describe how extinction adversely affects both biological and genetic diversity.

3. Identify the terms: "charismatic megafauna" and "flagship species."

4. Detail the cultural activities which affect biological resources.

5. List the direct/indirect benefits of preserving biological resources and diversity.

6. Describe how various cultures have historically managed exotic plants and animals.

7. Compare/contrast the variety of methods employed by both The Center for Plant Conservation and The Kew Botanical Gardens as they strive to preserve plant species.

8. List the four objectives associated with progressive zoos.

9. Identify the objectives associated with captive breeding, and the non-traditional breeding methods employed by zoos today.

10. List the pros/cons associated with both off- and on-site preservation.

11. Trace the history of American legislative efforts designed to manage our nation's biological resources.

12. Identify the following international attempts to preserve biological resources: Man and the Biosphere Program (MAB) and The Convention on International Trade in Endangered Species of Wild Flora and Fauna (CITES).

13. Define and identify the importance of the American Association of Zoological Parks and Aquariums (AAZPA) and the Species Survival Plan (SSP).

14. Identify what the officials at The St. Louis Zoo described as their most important goal in today's world.

> **Did You Know . . . ?**
>
> Fewer than one percent of the thousands of tropical plants have been studied for their possible medical use.

Key Concepts

Read this summary of Chapter 23 and identify the important concepts discussed in the chapter.

All species are biological resources. Biological diversity refers to the variety of life forms which inhabit the earth. Biological diversity is measured in terms of species diversity, the total number of species; ecosystem diversity, the variety of communities of organisms and their habitats; and genetic diversity, the variation among the members of a single population of a species. Each individual has a unique genotype, its composition of genes. The sum of all of the genes present in a population is a gene pool.

The number of species on earth today is unknown. Scientific estimates range from 3 million to 100 million. Only about 1.7 million species have actually been named, and just 3 percent of these have been studied. Also unknown is the rate of extinction, that is, how fast we are losing species. Extinction occurs when all individuals of a species are killed or die off; it diminishes biodiversity. While extinction is a natural process, human activities have greatly accelerated its rate in recent decades.

The planet's diverse ecosystems harbor millions of species. Endemic species are species unique to a particular ecosystem; they occur nowhere else on earth. The planet's most diverse ecosystems are the tropical rain forests and the ocean's coral reefs. The former is threatened by deforestation, conversion to agricultural land, roadbuilding, mining, and other development. Reefs are threatened by dynamiting, coral and shell collecting, siltation from streams and rivers flowing into the seas, and bleaching, which some researchers believe may be a result of global warming. Wetlands are also very diverse, and like rain forests and coral reefs, they are under great pressure, chiefly from development.

Social factors, particularly culturally inherited attitudes and beliefs about wild species, affect how we value, use, and manage biological resources. For example, endangered mammals or birds that are highly valued by humans are called "charismatic megafauna." Undesirable animals and plants are called vermin and weeds, respectively. Species hunted for sport are called game animals, while species not hunted for sport are called non-game animals. Most monies are directed at managing and protecting game animals and charismatic megafauna. Meanwhile, efforts to manage non-game animals and less "cuddly" species (like snakes or tortoises, for example) receive little funding.

Our attitudes and beliefs also give rise to many activities which threaten biological resources and biodiversity. The single greatest threat to wildlife is loss or degradation of habitat. Other activities that endanger biological resources are overharvesting and poaching and selective breeding. Why preserve diversity? The arguments can be grouped into five broad categories: indirect benefits (ecosystem services); direct benefits (agriculture, medicine, and industry); aesthetics; ethical considerations; and evolutionary potential.

Humans have been managing plant and animal species for thousands of years. From China to Egypt to South America, the collection of wild animals and plants by rulers and the elite were fairly common. Zoos originated in Europe, an off-shoot of game reserves. Their chief purpose was entertainment. Current efforts to manage biological resources concentrate on preserving plant and animal species or their genetic material, known as germplasm. Both species and germplasm may be preserved outside of their natural habitat in private collections, wildlife refuges, zoological parks, and seed or gene banks. Those who attempt to breed wild animals in captivity strive to maximize the contribution of unrelated animals in order to reduce the effects of inbreeding, and to attain a good age distribution in order to ensure a consistent number of individuals of breeding age. There are numerous advantages to off-site preservation. For many species, preservation in a zoo or botanical garden offers its best or only hope for long-term survival. In some cases, species may be preserved off-site until a time when they can be reintroduced to the wild. Off-site institutions also play a vital educational role; both adults and children learn about wildlife mainly through zoos. The most obvious disadvantage of off-site preservation is that it is an alternative only for those species known to us. It is also very expensive, and only a relatively small number of species can be preserved in zoos, botanical gardens, and gene banks because of space limitations. Further, in their natural habitat, species generally adapt to environmental changes. Sustained preservation of a species off-site reduces the likelihood of its successful reintroduction to the wild. In addition, we lack the basic biological knowledge needed to effectively manage and breed many exotic species. Finally, preserving species off-site ignores the other components of their ecosystems.

On-site preservation is accomplished through the establishment of national parks, protected wilderness areas, and biosphere reserves. It offers numerous advantages. Chief among these is that on-site preservation protects the entire ecosystem, both known and unknown species _and the relationships between them_. It holds out the best hope for preserving most species and for preserving maximum biological diversity. On-site preservation also allows a species to evolve with its environment. It is generally less expensive than off-site preservation, although protecting the designated preserve against poachers and development can greatly increase the cost.

Historically, most management efforts in the United States were aimed at game species, such as large mammals hunted for their horns or skins (furs) or large birds killed for their plumage. Most legislation dealt with the trade or transport of wild animals or animal products and thus did not protect living animals and their habitats. Moreover, such legislation ignored threatened plant species. The Endangered Species Act of 1973 marked a change in philosophy; it acknowledged the need to protect a diversity of species (plant and animal) as well as habitats.

235

Weaknesses of the law include: listing a species as threatened or endangered is expensive and time-consuming; there are not enough monies provided to adequately study and list all rare species; priority is given to mammals and more highly-visible creatures; and the listing process can be circumvented by the "God Committee," which can reverse the Fish and Wildlife Service's decision to protect endangered species.

At the international level, many countries have adopted various international treaties and conventions to protect migratory species. For the most part, these treaties have been bilateral agreements and have involved only a few countries in a specific region. One treaty, however, is global in nature. CITES, the Convention on International Trade in Endangered Species of Wild Flora and Fauna, protects threatened plants and animals worldwide and governs international trade in wildlife and wildlife products. Weaknesses of CITES include: some countries (such as China, a major importer of wildlife products) have not joined CITES and thus do not adhere to its decisions; signatory countries can ignore a CITES injunction simply by taking out a "reservation" on a species; and enforcement varies widely from country to country.

Key Terms

biodiversity

biological diversity

biological resource

charismatic megafauna

ecosystem diversity

endemic species

game animal

gene

gene pool

genetic diversity

genetic erosion

genotype

germplasm

minimum viable population size

non-game animal

species diversity

vermin

weed

Environmental Success Story

As a rubber tapper, Chico Mendes realized the importance of developing sustainable products, and he worked very hard to end the destruction of the Brazilian rainforest that was his home. He pioneered the creation of extractive reserves and openly opposed the cattle barons who were burning the forest. For all of his work for the rainforest, he was brutally gunned down outside his home in December 1988. But Mendes' story is a success, because before his death he was able to focus the world's attention on the threatened rain forest and the plight of indigenous peoples. His legacy still lives on; he has been called "the world's most celebrated environmental martyr" and received the Better World Society's Environmental Award.

True/False

1. The megadiversity countries are so called because of their great species diversity.   T   F

2. Because humans value domesticated species, extinction is not a threat to livestock.   T   F

3. About 10% of the earth's land surface is protected habitat (e.g., parks and reserves).   T   F

4. The Lacey Act prohibits imports of illegally killed animals.   T   F

5. There are approximately 1.4 million species on earth.   T   F

Fill in the Blank

1. The variation among members of a single population is called _____.

2. _____ is a term for loss of genetic variability in a population.

3. The use of _____ instead of traditional or wild strains contributes to the loss of genetic diversity in agriculture.

4. The _____ are typically large, attractive mammals which are popular with the general public; their management and protection are well-funded.

5. _____ are strains of plant species that have been bred for many years and handed down from generation to generation; they possess very specific traits (especially good flavor, for example, or hardiness) and are suited to specific areas or regions.

Multiple Choice

Choose the best answer.

1. The hereditary material of an organism is known as its
   A. gene pool.
   B. genetic variation.
   C. genotype.
   D. germplasm.

2. An endemic species is one that
   A. occurs in only one area.
   B. cannot survive in simulated natural habitats.
   C. is introduced to an area in which it not native.
   D. none of the above is true.

3. The most serious threat facing wildlife is
   A. poaching.
   B. overharvesting.
   C. habitat loss.
   D. selective breeding.

4. Zebra mussels in the Great Lakes are an example of a(n)
   A. charismatic megafauna.
   B. endangered species.
   C. endemic species.
   D. exotic species.

5. The dominant type of coastal wetland in tropical and subtropical regions is the
   A. bog.
   B. mangrove swamp.
   C. estuary.
   D. oxbow.

Short Answer

1. How many species inhabit the earth?

2. Which two types of ecosystems have the greatest species diversity?

3. Explain the terms "charismatic megafauna" and "vermin." To what do they refer and what does each term imply?

4. List and briefly describe three ways that zoos group animals.

5. What is ISIS?

Thought Questions

Develop a complete answer for each of the following.

1. Discuss how human culture and beliefs affect which species are valued and protected.

2. Describe how human activities threaten biological diversity.

3. Explain the arguments for preserving biological resources and maintaining biological diversity.

4. How do the zoos of today differ from the zoos of the past? Discuss how the reasons for collecting plant and animal species have changed over time.

5. Compare off-site and on-site preservation. Explain their differences in terms of species, ecosystem, and genetic diversity.

6. Describe the challenges faced by captive breeding programs.

7. Discuss the strengths and weaknesses of U.S. legislation designed to preserve biological diversity.

Related Concepts

Describe the relationship. (There may be more than one.)

BETWEEN...	AND...
extinction	ecosystem diversity
genetic diversity	species diversity
heirloom variety	genetic erosion
international wildlife trade	CITES
species	ecosystems

Did You Know ...?

Cortisone, a drug for skin irritations and Diosgenin, the active ingredient in birth control pills, were derived from plants found in Mexican and Guatemalan rainforests.

Suggested Activities

1. Find out what your local zoo is doing to preserve biological diversity. Volunteer to help with an activity or event that intrigues you.

2. Put up a bird house or bird bath. Observe the species that visit.

3. If you have a garden, experiment with growing heirloom or traditional varieties.

CHAPTER 24

Cultural Resources

Chapter Outline

I. Describing Cultural Resources

    A. Physical and Biological Boundaries

        1. What Are Cultural Resources?

        2. Where Are Cultural Resources Found?

    B. Social Boundaries

        1. Why Are Cultural Resources Significant?

            a. Historical Record of Societies and Their Environments

            b. Symbols of Our Heritage

            c. Cultural Identity

            d. Storehouse of Environmental Knowledge

            e. Economic Benefits

        2. What Are the Threats to Cultural Resources?

II. History of Management of Cultural Resources

    A. How Have Cultural Resources Been Preserved in the United States?

        1. Early Government Involvement in the Preservation of Cultural Resources

        2. Effects of World War II and Postwar Economic Growth on Preservation of Cultural Resources

3. Major Efforts to Preserve Cultural Resources Since 1960

   B. How Are Cultural Resources Preserved Worldwide?

III. Future Management of Cultural Resources

   A. Prevent Abuse of Cultural Resources

   B. Safeguard Cultural Resources Worldwide

   C. Preserve Cultural Resources as Part of Living Systems

Learning Objectives

After learning the material in Chapter 24 you should be able to:

1. Define cultural resource, including material and nonmaterial cultures in your definition.

2. List the reasons why cultural resources are considered to be significant.

3. Describe the variety of internal and external threats to cultural resources.

4. Identify the multiple reasons why vandalism is considered to be damaging.

5. Detail the reasons why acculturation is considered to be the greatest threat to nonmaterial cultural resources.

6. Trace the history of legislation designed to safeguard cultural resources in the United States.

7. List the different methods one can employ to initiate urban revival activities.

8. Identify the three conventions passed by UNESCO as a means of protecting global cultural heritage.

9. Trace the history of the Statue of Liberty as a National Monument, and identify the means by which restoration of this statue was achieved.

Did You Know . . . ?

Thirty-one wars were being fought in 1991, down from 36 in 1986.

Key Concepts

Read this summary of Chapter 24 and identify the important concepts discussed in the chapter.

A cultural resource is anything that embodies or represents a part of the culture of a specific people. All cultural resources arise from human thought or action. They often reflect or are part of the environment. Material cultural resources are tangible objects -- tools, furniture, monuments, and artwork, for example -- that humans create to make life easier or more enjoyable. Nonmaterial cultural resources include intangible objects such as traditions, customs, and folklore. Cultural resources management is concerned with preserving both material and living culture.

Cultural resources can be found virtually everywhere. They are significant because they provide us with a record of societies and their environments, are symbols of our heritage, are integral to cultural identity, are a valuable storehouse of environmental knowledge, provide economic benefits, and are essential for cultural diversity. Material cultural resources may be damaged because of the location of a structure, the ground on which it sits, the soil type, faulty materials, and building defects. They may also be damaged by long-term natural causes (rain, frost, humidity, vining vegetation, and animal droppings, for example). Air pollution, the use of wells, and the construction of tunnels can also threaten material culture. Others factors that may damage material culture include changing tastes in fashion, war, development, vandalism, looting, and pillaging. The greatest threat to nonmaterial culture is acculturation, the process by which one culture adapts or is modified through contact with another.

Until fairly recently the private sector was the force behind the preservation movement in the United States. The Antiquities Act of 1906 was the country's first major piece of legislation to safeguard cultural resources. The chief international agency working to protect the global cultural heritage is UNESCO, the United Nations Educational, Scientific, and Cultural Organization. UNESCO member nations agree to a binding legal framework that obliges them to protect the global cultural heritage. UNESCO can establish international conventions concerning the protection of cultural resources. Countries are free to ratify a convention or not, as they choose, but if they do ratify it, they are bound to comply with its stipulations. So far, UNESCO has enacted three conventions. One concerns the protection of cultural resources in case of an armed conflict, another establishes guidelines to prohibit and prevent the illegal import, export, and transfer of ownership of cultural resources. The third establishes the World Heritage List of objects and sites of global importance.

Key Terms

acculturation

cultural resource

cultural resources management

historic preservation

living culture

material culture

nonmaterial culture

rehabilitation

restoration

urban renewal

urban revival

Environmental Success Story

When most schoolchildren get back their graded assignments and tests, they just throw them away. Now, however, more and more schools are setting up programs so the students can recycle. Here are a few examples: The School Paper Recycling Project in New York City can take credit for keeping five tons of paper out of landfills; 16 Ontario schools, soon to be followed by every other school in the 290 Ontario communities, recycle cans, bottles, and paper; and students from public schools in Berkeley, California saved more than a ton of paper.

True/False

1. Material culture includes such things as language, customs,   T   F
    traditions, and folklore.

2. Indigenous or tribal people tend to possess a broad and deep   T   F
    knowledge of their ecosystems.

3. The outward features of a culture can be abandoned more   T   F
    easily than can cultural knowledge and values.

4. Both material and nonmaterial cultural resources are   T   F
    threatened by extrinsic factors.

5. Until fairly recently, the federal government was responsible T   F
    for most historic preservation in the United States.

Fill in the Blank

1. _____ is the field concerned with preserving material
    cultural resources.

2. Folklore is an example of _____ culture.

3. _____ is the process by which one culture adapts or is modified
    through contact with another.

4. Faulty building materials and design defects are examples of _____ threats.

5. The National Historic Preservation Act created the _____,
    a list of historic sites of local, state, and regional significance.

Short Answer

1. What is the difference between historic preservation and cultural resources
    management?

2. Explain how acid precipitation threatens material cultural resources.

245

3. What 1906 legislation gave the president the power to designate national monuments?

4. What is UNESCO?

5. What is the World Heritage List?

Thought Questions

Develop a complete answer for each of the following.

1. Why are cultural resources important and worthy of preservation? List and explain at least five reasons. Are there any arguments for not preserving them?

2. What factors threaten both material and nonmaterial culture? List and describe at least seven.

3. What is the connection between cultural resources and the environment? Between the study of cultural resources and environmental science? Are cultural resources an appropriate topic in an environmental science text? Why or why not?

4. Briefly summarize the history of cultural resources preservation in the United States. What forces gave rise to the modern preservation movement?

5. What is being done to preserve cultural resources in the United States and worldwide? What are the major organizations and legislation involved?

Related Concepts

Describe the relationship. (There may be more than one.)

BETWEEN...	AND...
acculturation	native Americans
acid precipitation	extrinsic threat
pillaging for profit	Archeological Resources Protection Act of 1979
urban renewal	historic preservation
cultural resources	environment

Did You Know . . . ?

Americans throw out two billion disposable razors each year.

Suggested Activities

1. Discover the past of a historic site.

2. Visit a natural history museum or historical society.

3. Learn about the customs of a culture other than your own.

4. Study the history and customs of your own family. Talk to relatives to find out where these traditions came from.

UNIT SEVEN

AN ENVIRONMENTAL LEGACY

CHAPTER 25

Religion and Ethics

Chapter Outline

I. What is Religion?

    A. Expression of the Human Belief In and Reverence For a Superhuman Power

    B. Characterized by Core of Beliefs which Answer Questions about God, World

    C. Two Important Religious Questions Reiterate Humanity's Place in World

        1. Are Humans Part Of, or Apart From, Nature?

        2. What is Humanity's Role in Creation; to Act as Master or as Steward?

II. How Does Religion Affect Environmental Problem Solving and Management?

    A. Belief that God Will Solve All Earthly Problems

        1. Inspires a Sense of Security

        2. May Cause Humans to Delay Action on Environmental Concerns

    B. Limit Options Available to Followers Struggling with Environmental Problem

    C. May Encourage Anthropocentric View

        1. Humans Are Preeminent in Creation

        2. Affects Choices or Solutions to an Environmental Problem

    D. Can Foster a Biocentric World View

        1. Translates into Care and Concern for Other Species

2. Consideration for the Health and Balance of the Natural World

III. How Are Religions Promoting Environmentally Sound Management?

A. Some Modern Examples

1. North American Conference on Christianity (NACCE) founded in 1986

2. The Eleventh Commandment Fellowship

3. The Franciscan Center for Environmental Studies Opened in 1988

4. Representatives to Five Major Religions Met in 1988 to Pledge Support for Conservation

5. Earth-based Spiritualities and Traditions Becoming More Popular

B. Saint Francis of Assisi -- Monk Whose Lifestyle Exemplified that of a Steward of Nature

1. Defined Cornerstones of Franciscan Order of Catholic Monks

2. Based His Care for Living Things on Two Concepts

a. Anything Created by God Should Remind Us of Him

b. Things Worthy of Special Love Because They Symbolize Character of God

3. Author of "The Canticle of Brother Sun," Celebrating Brotherhood of All

C. The Amish Communities

1. A Protestant Group Exemplifying Environmentally Sound Living

2. Practice Labor-Intensive, Low-Input Farming

3. Family Farms Utilize

a. Animal Labor

b. Organic Farming Techniques

IV. What Are Ethics?

A. Branch of Philosophy Concerned with Standards of Conduct and Moral Judgment

B. System/Code Which Shapes Attitudes/Behavior Toward Others and the World

V. How Do Ethics Affect Environmental Problem Solving and Management?

    A. "Frontier Ethic"

        1. Began with Judeo-Christian "Biblical Mandate" Condoning Resource Use

        2. Land and Natural Resources Exploited Without Regard for Ecosystem

    B. Consumer Lifestyle a Cause of Many Current Environmental Problems

    C. Stewardship Ethic -- Humans in the Role of Caretakers of the Natural World

    D. Land Ethic

        1. First Formal Statement of an Environmental Ethic

        2. Developed Approximately Fifty Years Ago by Aldo Leopold

        3. Defined as the Limitation of Freedom in the Struggle for Existence

        4. Expands Definition of Community to Include Soils, Water

        5. Reaffirms the Right of Natural Resources to Exist

VI. How Can We Apply a Personal Ethic to Societal Problems?

    A. Variability of Personal Ethics Makes Them Difficult to Apply to Societal Problems

    B. Examples of Environmental Subjects Raising Ethical Questions

        1. California Condors Removed from Wild for Captive Propagation

        2. Pacific Yew -- Slow-Growing Tree Found in Old-Growth Forests which Contains Cancer-Fighting Substance

3. Genetic Engineering -- Questions on Constructive/Destructive Possibilities

Learning Objectives

After learning the material in Chapter 25 you should be able to:

1. Define religion and the two important religious teachings which concern humanity's place in the scheme of the world.

2. Describe how religion affects environmental problem solving and management.

3. Describe the various ways by which religions are promoting environmentally sound management.

4. Identify Saint Francis of Assisi, the two concepts which he identified as being the focus of life and its creation, and "The Canticle of Brother Sun."

5. Explain the difference between ethics and morals.

6. Determine the various ways by which ethics affects environmental problem solving and management.

7. Explain the meanings of environmental ethic and stewardship.

8. Identify Aldo Leopold and the "land ethic."

9. Describe the Eleventh Commandment and its message to humankind.

Did You Know . . . ?

Some communities in the United States pay more to get rid of their trash than to maintain their police departments.

Key Concepts

Read this summary of Chapter 25 and identify the important concepts discussed in the chapter.

Religion is the expression of human belief in and reverence for a superhuman power recognized as a supreme being, a supernatural realm, or an ultimate meaning. Religions are characterized by a unique core of beliefs or teachings that answer basic questions about the universe, existence, the world, and humankind. The values, beliefs, and attitudes inspired by religions affect, to varying degrees, how the faithful respond to specific environmental concerns. Religion is an important component of a people's worldview.

Religions can affect environmental problem solving and management in several ways: by preventing people from taking action on problems in the belief that God will take care of all things; limiting the actions or options of its followers in a given situation; and shaping followers' worldviews (which affect beliefs, values, attitudes, and behavior).

The past few decades have seen a shift in the thinking of some organized religions. Concern for the earth and the belief that humans are to act as stewards of creation are increasingly widespread ideas among many religious groups.

Ethics is a branch of philosophy concerned with standards of conduct and moral judgment. An ethic is a system or code of morals -- principles that help us to distinguish right from wrong -- that shapes attitudes and behavior. Aldo Leopold, in *A Sand County Almanac*, maintained that ethics should be extended from their purely social context to the land and environment. He argued for the development of a land ethic to guide our behavior toward the environment. Such an ethic, he maintained, would transform humans from conquerors of the biotic community to "plain member and citizen of it." Leopold pointed out than a land ethic would imply respect for the biotic community and the environment as a whole.

There is no universal human ethic. Moreover, ethical codes change over time; what seems correct and appropriate in one era may be viewed as immoral in another. For example, the frontier ethic, which fostered aggressive behavior toward the environment, is gradually being replaced by a stewardship ethic, in which humans are seen as caretakers of the natural world. The stewardship ethic is a type of land ethic.

The Eleventh Commandment Fellowship offers suggestions for developing and implementing a personal environmental ethic. But it is difficult to apply our ethical standards in societal situations because many people have widely different ideas about what is ethical behavior, and in many societal issues there is no clear-cut right and wrong. In the case of the California condor, the Pacific yew tree and gene engineering, there is an ongoing debate to decide how we as a society should proceed.

Key Terms

anthropocentric worldview

biocentric worldview

environmental ethic

ethics

ethic

frontier ethic

land ethic

morals

stewardship ethic

Environmental Success Story

When the nearby sewage treatment plant was faced with too much waste to handle, the Ben & Jerry's Homemade Ice Cream plant decided to help by diverting some of its milky waste to somewhere different. This most unusual place was a pig farm. The company bought 250 piglets for the farmer while providing him with the solids from the milk to prepare the pigs for market. The only condition that the farmer had to agree to was to name three of his pigs Ben, Jerry, and Ed Stanek. Ed is the head of Vermont's Environmental Commission and a supporter of this waste reduction method.

True/False

1. About one-third of the world's population profess beliefs in   T   F
    some form of Christianity.

2. The frontier ethic was the first formally developed statement T   F
    of an environmental ethic.

3. A stewardship ethic may be based on either a biocentric or   T   F
    anthropocentric worldview.

4. Ethics place limits on human actions.   T   F

5. Religions do not affect how people solve environmental   T   F
    problems and manage resources.

Fill in the Blank

1. Aldo Leopold promoted a(n) _____ ethic in his book, *A Sand County Almanac.*

2. The belief that a divine entity is embodied in the living world is known as _____.

3. The _____ are a Protestant group that practices low-input agriculture and self-reliant living.

4. The _____ ethic encourages the exploitation of natural resources.

5. The _____ has been found to contain taxol, a cancer-fighting agent.

Multiple Choice

Choose the best answer.

1. St. Francis of Assisi has been proposed as the Patron Saint of
   A. ethics.
   B. religion.
   C. ecology.
   D. Italy.

2. A moral is a(n)
   A. ending to a story.
   B. principle that helps an individual distinguish right from wrong.
   C. majority, in some cases.
   D. ethical decision.

3. Fundamental physical units of heredity that transmit information from one cell to another and thereby from one generation to another are
   A. bacteria.
   B. one-celled organisms.
   C. plasma.
   D. genes.

4. According to Edward Abbey, the "conscience of our race" is
   A. absent.
   B. ecology.
   C. environmentalism.
   D. ethics.

5. The two core concepts central to all earth-based spiritualities are:
   A. immanence and interconnection.
   B. stewardship and anthropocentrism.
   C. stewardship and biocentrism.
   D. feminism and rebirth.

Short Answer

1. What factors other than religious tenets play a role in determining people's behavior toward the environment?

2. What is the Eleventh Commandment Fellowship?

3. List three traditions of earth-based spiritualities.

4. What is an ethic?

5. What is the significance of the bacterium *Escherichia coli*?

Thought Questions

Develop a complete answer for each of the following.

1. Discuss how religious beliefs and ethical codes affect the environment.

2. How are organized religions dealing with the environmental question today? In what ways are they promoting environmentally sound management?

3. Do anthropocentric worldviews always result in non-sustainable systems or harmful effects on the environment? Explain your answer.

4. Discuss why it is difficult to apply personal ethical codes to social problems.

5. Explain the genetic engineering controversy. Give examples of possible beneficial and destructive uses of this technology.

Related Concepts

Describe the relationship. (There may be more than one.)

BETWEEN...	AND...
anthropocentrism	ecosystem balance
earth-based spirituality	biocentrism
stewardship ethic	Saint Francis of Assisi
exploitation	wise use
California condor	habitat loss

Did You Know . . . ?

As of 1990, 70 percent of religious denominations were committed to environmental causes.

Suggested Activities

1. Study the sacred texts of a religion that you follow or are interested in. What do they teach about the relationship between humans and nature?

2. Become familiar with ecologically appropriate techniques, practices, and devices, and find ways to use them in your own life. For example, start a compost heap in your backyard or neighborhood.

3. Study the life and works of a naturalist, such as Saint Francis of Assisi, Aldo Leopold, Rachel Carson, or John Muir.

CHAPTER 26

Economics and Politics

Chapter Outline

I. What Is the Study of Economics?

    A. Study of How We Manage and Organize Our Home and Its Many Resources

    B. Usually Focuses on Price of the Earth's Resources Rather Than Its Value

    C. Environmental/Resource Usage Problems Often Result of Emphasis on Price

II. How Does Economics Affect Environmental Problem Solving and Management?

    A. Environmental Problem Solving

        1. Alternative Solutions Often Compared to Determine Most Cost-Effective

        2. Cost Often Viewed as the Primary Determinant of the Solution

    B. Environmental Management

        1. Renewable Resources Can Yield Sustained Economic Benefits

        2. Nonrenewable Resources Are Limited in Availability and Useful Quality

        3. Throughout History of U.S., Economy Stressed Resource Utilization/Conservation

        4. National Economies Can Be Improved by Using Resources More Efficiently

III. How Are Economic Programs Contributing to Environmentally Sound Management?

    A. People Are Becoming Aware of the Link Between Sound Environmental Policies and Sound Economics

    B. Examples of National and International Initiatives to Link Economics and Environmental Protection

IV. The World Debt Crisis

    A.   Banks Have Loaned Billions to LDCs for Use in Development Projects Intended To:

        1. Alleviate Poverty

        2. Increase National Viability in World Market

    B. Nations Left Without Enough Money to Simply Pay Interest on Loans

    C. Unsuccessful Development of Large Projects Has Decreased Standard of Living

    D. Result: Woes Increase Occurrence of Such Degrading Activities as Deforestation

    E. Questions Plaguing Third World

        1. How to Reduce the Potentially Adverse Impacts of Development Projects

        2. Provide for Management of Renewable Resources to Ensure Sustainability

    F. Possible Solutions

        1. Encourage Banks to Become Responsible by Investing In Only Sound Practices

        2. Encourage Developments that Maximize Human/Wealth Potential

        3. Encourage Grass Roots Loans that Invest In the People, Not Projects

4. Swap Huge Debts for the Establishment and Protection of Nature Reserves

V. What Is Politics?

    A. Definition
       1. Encompasses the Principles, Policies, and Programs of Government

       2. Different Political Systems are Based on Different Principles

    B. Politics Affects Problem Solving -- Reflects Lack of Political Will to Take On the Issues

    C. Political Decisions Often Affect How Resources Are Managed

    D. Political Programs Contribute to Environmentally Sound Management (Antarctic Bill)

Learning Objectives

After learning the material in Chapter 26 you should be able to:

1. Explain the difference between value and price as it applies to resources.

2. Describe the relationship between environmentally sound management and economics.

3. Discuss the world debt crisis and explain how it relates to environmental problems.

4. Explain the relationship between politics and solutions to environmental problems, giving both national and international examples.

Did You Know. . . ?

In 1990 the United States spent $303 billion to protect against military threats, but only $14 billion on environmental threats--a ratio of 22 to 1.

Key Concepts

Read this summary of Chapter 26 and identify the important concepts discussed in the chapter.

Economics and politics have a significant amount of influence over the resources to which we have access and the measures we use to solve environmental problems and manage resources.

Economics is the study of the management of the household -- a state, nation, or the world at large. There is a great difference between a resource's value and its price. If, as a society, we were to realize the true value of our resources, we could avoid many of our environmental problems.

Economic considerations are an integral part of problem solving. Proposed alternative solutions are often compared to determine which solution is more cost-effective. Unfortunately, economic cost is often viewed as the sole or primary determinant in the selection of a response to an environmental problem. Economic analysis is also a criterion for environmentally sound management. For most of the history of the United States, our economic system has stressed resource utilization over conservation. Increasingly, people are realizing the important link between sound environmental policies and sound economics. Fees on chemical use, well construction, and other activities are being instituted to protect groundwater; green taxes are being implemented to achieve other environmental quality objectives.

Many less-developed countries have gone into debt from large-scale development projects such as dams and major roadways. Many are unable to pay even the interest on these loans. However, the loans have not helped improve economics conditions for citizens, and economic woes intensify environmental degradation. Some solutions to the debt crisis are to require that lending institutions act more responsibly with respect to projects that affect the environment; to promote sustainable development (improving the quality of human life while living within the carrying capacity of supporting ecosystems); to increase and rechannel development assistance by MDCs to LDCs; to provide grassroots loans to individuals or groups for small, sustainable development projects; and to encourage debt-for-nature swaps. These solutions can help to achieve a sustainable economy, one which maintains its natural resource base, and a sustainable society, a society that works with, not against, natural systems.

Different political systems are based on different principles, and they adopt different policies and programs in order to govern their societies. Even within a particular nation, all citizens do not agree on the best means of government. History has shown that concern for the environment is not the sole domain for any major national political party.

Lack of political will prevents us from alleviating or eliminating many serious environmental problems. The political will to take action on issues usually stems from sufficient public demand. Politics is an important component of international environmental issues as well as national ones.

Political decisions often affect how resources are managed. Antarctica provides one timely example of the impact of politics. Just as economics can contribute to environmentally sound resource management, politics, too, holds the potential for much environmental good.

Key Terms

debt-for-nature swap

economics

politics

price

sustainable development

sustainable economy

sustainable society

sustainable use

value

Environmental Success Story

In today's technical world, one answer to our waste management problem is an electronic marketplace for companies to deal with their waste. TEAM-W, which stands for "The Electronic Answer for Managing Waste," was established by Cincinnati Bell Laboratory. It serves as a computer bulletin board and is founded on the principal that one company's waste might be viewed as a raw material to be used by another company. Things seem to be going well for the company, considering that over 80 percent of the 14,000 companies contacted have requested more information.

True/False

1. In terms of percentage of GNP, Norway contributes the   T   F
   highest level of non-military assistance to developing
   countries.

2. The largest volume of debt-for-nature swaps has been made   T   F
   by Bolivia.

3. The Green Belt and Chipko movements are both concerned   T   F
   with preserving trees.

4. The Antarctic continent is a desert, receiving less than 3   T   F
   inches of precipitation annually.

5. All resources can be used on a sustainable basis.   T   F

Fill in the Blank

1. The largest lending institution in the world is _____.

2. _____ seeks to manage natural, human, and
   physical resources to serve the common good.

3. Sustainable use does not apply to _____ resources.

4. The only industry in Antarctica is _____.

5. In a _____, a conservation organization "buys" a portion of the
   debt of a nation at a discount from the bank that made the loan; in exchange, the
   nation agrees to establish and protect a nature reserve or implement a
   conservation program.

Multiple Choice

Choose the best answer.

1. The Greek root word for both economics and ecology means
   A. value.
   B. earth.
   C. household.
   D. pride.

2. The world debt crisis illustrates how environmental degradation and ___are
   related.
   A. economic chaos

B. culture
C. disease
D. politics

3. _____is defined as improving the quality of human life while living within the carrying capacity of supporting ecosystems.
A. Environmental economics
B. Environmental management
C. Sustainable development
D. Sustainable economy

4. One of the most important topics of discussion at the Earth Summit in Rio de Janeiro was
A. overpopulation.
B. hunger.
C. world debt crisis.
D. global warming.

5. The only kind of resources that have been tapped in Antarctica are
A. fossil fuels.
B. minerals.
C. biological.
D. fresh water.

Short Answer

1. What is a green tax?

2. Define sustainable development.

3. What is the Hague Declaration?

4. Who owns Antarctica? Explain.

5. Define sustainable economy.

Thought Questions

Develop a complete answer for each of the following.

1. Discuss the differences between the Amish farm economy and mainstream U.S. agribusiness.

2. Explain how economics affects environmental management, and give two examples of how economic incentives are being used to encourage environmentally sound management.

3. Describe the impact of large-scale industrial projects on the economic and environmental health of LDCs.

4. Discuss how politics contributes to both environmental problems and their solutions.

5. How is Antarctica currently managed? What are the threats to the world's last pristine environment?

Related Concepts

Describe the relationship.   (There may be more than one.)

BETWEEN...	AND...
value	price
environmental degradation	economic chaos
World Bank	world debt crisis
ANILCA	Tongass Reform Act
sustainable economy	sustainable society

> **Did You Know ... ?**
>
> An estimated 14 million college students make up about 8 percent of the potential voting population. But so few Americans participate in national elections that

students could control as much as 20 percent of the vote. So vote!

Suggested Activities

1. Join an organization that lobbies to protect the environment.

2. Hold an environmental town meeting. Before a local, state, or national election, invite local candidates to the town meeting to discuss their environmental views.

3. Find out your legislators' records on environmental issues and write to them to show your support for the environment. You can find out how your member of Congress voted on key environmental legislation by reading *The National Environmental Scorecard*, a voting chart published every two years. The Scorecard can be obtained for $15 from the League of Conservation Voters, 2000 L St., NW, Suite 804, Washington, DC 20036.

4. Don't forget to vote!

CHAPTER 27

Law and Dispute Resolution

Chapter Outline

I. What Is Environmental Law?

    A. Definition

        1. Part of Legal System which Governs the Behavior of Private/Public Groups

        2. Regulates the Impact of Their Activities on Others and on Natural Resources

        3. Based on Two Types of Laws: Common and Statutory

    B. Common Law

        1. Written/Unwritten Principles Based on Past Legal Decisions, or Precedents

        2. Precedents, Balancing Competing Interests in Society, Based on Three Legal Torts

            a. Nuisance

                1. Most Common Ground for Action in the Field of Environmental Law

                2. Based on Wrongs which Arise from the Unreasonable Use of Property

                3. Settled by Compensation and/or Abatement

            b. Trespass

                1. When Someone Invades/Intrudes Upon Another's Property

                2. Must Have Proof of Intent or Reckless Action

    c. Negligence

        1. Person Acts in such a Manner that His or Her Action/Inaction Causes Damage

        2. Action/Lack of Action as Cause of Injury and Consequences Foreseeable

  3. Liability

    a. Once Harm Has Been Found, Liability Must Be Determined

    b. Strict Liability

        1. Of Particular Relevance to Environmental Law

        2. If Harm Results from a Product or Action, the Party that Made the Product or Performed the Action is Liable for the Harm Done, No Matter How Careful the Party Was and Even If the Results Can Be Considered Unforeseeable

C. Statutory Laws

  1. Passed By the State Legislature or Congress

  2. Governs How Environment/Human Health are Protected; Resources are Managed

II. How Are Environmental Laws Enforced?

  A. Each Law Specifies How and By Whom It Is To Be Enforced

  B. Environmental Protection Agency -- Federal Government's Primary "Environmental Watchdog"

  C. Each State Has Its Own Enforcement Agencies

  D. Enforcement Is Not Always Achieved

    1. Allocation of Authority May Be Unclear

2. Governing Agency May Disagree with the Principle or Intent of the Law

3. Congress/Administration May Fail to Apportion Funds for Its Enforcement

4. Agency May Have Conflicting Priorities

III. How Do Environmentally Sound Laws Contribute to Problem Solving and Management?

A. Disputes Arise When Parties Disagree Over Alternative Uses of Available Resources

B. Environmental Problem Solving -- Relevant Laws Can Be Guidelines to Finding Solutions

C. Environmentally Sound Resource Management -- Legal System Contributes in Subtle Ways

1. Stewardship Ethic -- Endangered Species Act

2. Biocentric Worldview -- Wilderness Act of 1964

3. Natural System Knowledge -- The Farm Act of 1985

4. Political System Knowledge -- Laws Enacted Only After Lobbying, Compromise

5. Sociocultural Considerations -- National Historic Preservation Act

6. Natural and Social System Research -- Environmental Impact Statements

7. Economic Analysis -- Laws Attempt To Put Monetary Value on Resources

8. Public Participation -- Laws Mandate Public Forums on Issues

9. Environmental Education -- Resource Conservation and Recovery Act

IV. How Is the Field of Environmental Law Changing?

A. Environmental Law Has Advanced Significantly Since the 1960s

B. Natural Resources Defense Council

　1. Initiated in 1970, Called the Most Effective Public Interest Lobbying Group

　2. Reputation Built On:

　　a. Series of Winning Law Suits

　　b. Forcing Agencies to Adopt Environmentally Safe Practices

C. Formation of the Virginia Environmental Endowment -- Innovative Legal Solution

　1. Result of Allied Chemical's $13 Million Fine for Polluting the James River

　2. Judge Accepted Allied's Proposal to Use $8 Million of Fine to Benefit People of Virginia

V. What Is Environmental Dispute Resolution?

A. Definition

　1. Process of Negotiation/Compromise when Disputing Parties Meet Face to Face

　2. Goal is to Reach a Mutually Acceptable Solution to a Problem

　3. Neutral Third Party, called Mediator, Facilitates Negotiations

　4. Mediator Cannot Impose Settlements

　5. Dispute Settled When Parties Reach What They Consider to be a Workable Solution

B. What are the Advantages and Disadvantages of Dispute Resolution?

　1. Advantages

　　a. Gives All Parties a Better Chance to Realize Objectives

　　b. Speed Solutions

　　c. Avoids the Cost of Litigation

271

2. Disadvantages

    a. Inadequate Funding for Negotiation Services

    b. Fear of Losing Power/Status by Negotiating Groups

    c. Lack of Faith in the Outcome of the Negotiations; Not Legally Enforceable

C. How Does Dispute Resolution Contribute to Environmental Problem Solving and Management?

    1. Disputing Parties Brought Together -- May Minimize Problems

    2. Coordinated Resource Management Planning -- Compromise

Learning Objectives

After learning the material in Chapter 27 you should be able to:

1. Define environmental law, and identify the two types of law most commonly associated with it.

2. Identify the four legal axioms, or torts, which are the basis for precedence.

3. Explain how laws are enforced, and why this enforcement is not always effective.

4. Determine the relationship between environmentally sound management and the law.

5. Identify the work accomplished by the Natural Resources Defense Council.

6. Describe how the Virginia Environmental Endowment Fund was created, exemplifying how judicial action can benefit the environment.

7. Define dispute resolution, the role of the mediator, and its associated advantages/disadvantages.

Did You Know . . . ?

In 1972 only 26 countries had environmental protection agencies. Today there are 161.

Key Concepts

Read this summary of Chapter 27 and identify the important concepts discussed in the chapter.

Environmental law governs the activities of persons, corporations, government agencies, and other public and private groups in order to regulate the impact of the activities on the environment and natural resources. Environmental protection resides in common and statutory law. Common law is a large body of written and unwritten principles and rules based on thousands of past legal decisions dating back to the beginning of the English legal system. It is built on precedent, a legal decision that may serve as an example, reason, or justification for a later decision. Cases involving common law are based on nuisance (a class of wrongs that arise from the unreasonable, unwarrantable, or unlawful use of a person's own property that produces annoyance, inconvenience, or material injury to another), trespass (unwarranted or uninvited entry upon another's property by a person, the person's agent, or an object that he or she caused to be deposited there), or negligence (the failure to exercise the care that "a prudent person" usually takes, resulting in an action or inaction that causes personal harm or property damage). Nuisance, trespass, and negligence are known as torts, causes of action (wrongful acts) for which a civil suit can be brought by an injured plaintiff against a defendant. An injunction is a court order to do or refrain from doing a specified act; an injunction that requires the defendant to stop or restrict the nuisance is called an abatement. Compensation is a monetary award for damages.

Statutory law is the body of law passed by a local legislature or Congress. Congress has enacted several important environmental and resource protection laws. Each environmental law specifies how it is to be enforced and who is to enforce it. The Environmental Protection Agency (EPA) is perhaps the best known of the federal agencies charged with enforcing environmental policies. Each state also has its own agencies.

Environmental laws are not always enforced effectively. Allocation of authority may be unclear. The agency charged with enforcing a law may disagree with the law. The administration or Congress may not provide the funds needed for enforcement. An agency may have a conflict of interest that keeps it from enforcing a law. Finally, the burden of administrative duties may hamper an agency's ability to enforce laws.

Environmentally sound laws are important to environmental problem solving and management. The legal system comes into play at each step of the problem-solving process. Environmental law has advanced significantly since the 1960s, when the first such federal laws were enacted. The earliest laws dealt with such things as point sources contributing to air and water pollution. Recent laws have focused

273

more on preventing pollution or resource abuse by promoting conservation measures.

Groups such as the Natural Resources Defense Council and creative legal decisions, such as the one that resulted in the creation of the Virginia Environmental Endowment, have helped the field of environmental law to change and grow. Even so, environmental law and litigation can not provide a satisfactory solution in every case or problem. In such instances, environmental dispute resolution may be helpful. Dispute resolution is the process of negotiation and compromise by which conflicting parties reach a mutually acceptable solution to a problem. A neutral third party called a mediator facilitates negotiations. Dispute resolution or negotiation offers several important advantages: it hastens resolution, generally costs less, and there is a better chance that all parties will realize their objectives and reach a satisfying solution. Disadvantages are: funding for negotiation services is inadequate, some parties fear that they will lose power or status by appearing to be willing to compromise, and some people lack faith in the outcome of negotiations, since they are not legally binding.

Key Terms

common law

compensation

dispute resolution

environmental law

injunction

mediator

negligence

nuisance

precedent

statutory law

strict liability

tort

trespass

Environmental Success Story

Instead of delivering barrels of sludge to corporate headquarters or plugging discharge pipes, Marco Kaltofen has found a more effective way of forcing companies to control their pollution. He lives in the Boston area and operates a chemical analysis laboratory for the National Toxics Campaign. He arms himself with a pH meter, a chemical analysis kit, plastic bags, empty bottles, and a notebook and heads out to gather information. When he is ready with his results, he publicizes his findings by calling a press conference. As a result of one of his successful investigations, American Cyanide pleaded guilty to 37 criminal counts of polluting the Rahway River and was fined $900,000. Because of the slow nature of the government, Kaltofen believes that citizens are more effective than the government agencies at enforcing environmental laws.

True/False

1. A person can be charged with trespass only if they themselves   T   F
    enter another person's property.

2. If harm results from a product, the maker of that product is not   T   F
    liable for the harm done if it (the result or harm) is determined
    to be unforeseeable.

3. Statutory laws are derived from precedent.   T   F

4. Dispute resolution relies upon negotiation and compromise.   T   F

5. A legal decision that serves as an example, reason, or   T   F
    justification for a late decision is known as a prior restraint.

Fill in the Blank

1. Two methods for settling environmental disputes are _____
    and _____ .

2. In 1970, President Nixon created the _____ to enforce
    environmental laws.

3. The most common cause of action in environmental law is _____ .

4. In dispute resolution, the disputing parties are assisted by a neutral third party,
    called a(n) _____ .

5. A large body of written and unwritten principles and rules based on thousands of
    past legal decisions dating back to the beginning of the English legal system is

------------------.

Multiple Choice

Choose the best answer.

1. A monetary award for damages is called
   A. fee.
   B. litigation.
   C. abatement.
   D. compensation.

2. The failure to exercise care that a "prudent person" usually takes, resulting in an action or inaction that causes personal harm or property damage is called
   A. nuisance.
   B. trespass.
   C. negligence.
   D. liability.

3. A court order to do or refrain from doing a specified action is a(n)
   A. legal writ.
   B. abatement.
   C. precedent.
   D. injunction.

4. An alternative to legislation that relies upon compromise and negotiation between opposing factions is called
   A. coordinated resource management planning.
   B. teamwork.
   C. common law.
   D. statutory law.

5. Because of its work in helping to enforce environmental laws, the NRDC has been called a(n)
   A. shadow EPA.
   B. pain in the ---.
   C. environmental mediator.
   D. dispute resolver.

Short Answer

1. What is an abatement and what is it an example of?

2. List and briefly describe the three causes of action upon which cases involving common law are based.

3. Define nuisance and give an example.

4. Define negligence and give an example.

5. What is coordinated resource management planning?

Thought Questions

Develop a complete answer for each of the following.

1. Why are environmental laws not always effectively enforced?

2. Discuss how the legal system contributes to environmentally sound resource management.

3. What role does law play in environmental problem solving?

4. Re-read the section on the Virginia Environmental Endowment, and let it inspire you. Now, brainstorm some positive, creative, and constructive ways that polluters might be made to compensate society for the pollution they have caused.

5. Define dispute resolution and explain why many people are beginning to use it as an alternative to litigation. What are its advantages and disadvantages?

Related Concepts

Describe the relationship. (There may be more than one.)

BETWEEN...	AND...
common law	statutory law
biocentric worldview	Wilderness Act of 1964
National Resources Defense Council	Environmental Protection Agency
negligence	liability

dispute resolution	coordinated resource management planning

Did You Know . . . ?

Since 1986, Norway has increased its budget for environmental programs by 60 percent.

Suggested Activities

1. Find out who enforces environmental laws in your county or state and what means they use to ensure compliance.

2. Join a public interest organization that litigates on environmental issues.

3. Find out more about the programs developed by the Virginia Environmental Endowment, and look for opportunities to reapply them to problems in your area.

4. Try this role playing exercise: Form a coordinated resource management planning team with other members of your class. Adopting the roles of different types of resource managers and users, work together to develop a management plan for the resource of your choice.

CHAPTER 28

Environmental Education

Chapter Outline

I. What Is Environmental Education?

    A. Definition

        1. Goals as Stated in the First Issue of the *Environmental Education*

            a. Aimed at Producing Citizenry that is Knowledgeable Concerning the Environment

            b. Should Make People Aware of Environmental Problems and How to Help Solve Them

            c. Should Motivate People to Work Toward Their Solutions

        2. Goals Outlined in 1977 by The World Intergovernmental Conference

            a. To Develop Citizenry that is Aware Of and Concerned About Environment

            b. To Foster Knowledge, Motivation, Commitment to Work Toward Solutions of Problems

            c. To Encourage People to Apply Same Level of Commitment to Preventing New Problems

        3. Majority of EE Programs Foster Environmental Awareness Rather Than Problem Solving

        4. Broad Goals for Curriculum Development in Environmental Education Include:

            a. Ecological Foundations (Programs Based on Natural Science)

            b. Conceptual Awareness (Issues and Values)

c. Issue Investigation and Evaluation

d. Environmental Action Skills (Training and Application)

5. Goals of EE are Interrelated and Compatible -- Aid in Standardizing Holistic Experiences

6. Life-Long Educational Process

B. How Is Environmental Education Taught Formally?

1. Two Approaches

a. Teaching EE as a Separate Course

1. "Unrelated" Teachers Would Be Virtually Unaffected By Addition to Course Work

2. Disadvantage

a. Inability to Perceive Interconnectedness

b. Need Connection With Principles and How They Relate To Their Daily Lives

2. Teaching EE as an Integral Part of All Courses, as Appropriate for Class

a. Oak Park-River Forest High School -- Students Took On Responsibility for Environmental Education, Impacting Curriculum of Entire School

C. How is Environmental Education Taught Informally?

1. Examples of Organizations/Forums

a. Zoos, Nature Centers, Museums, Aquariums, and Wildlife Refuges

b. National and International Environmental Organizations

c. Nonprofit Corporations

2. EE More Than a Passing Movement, but More Effort Needed to Weave It Throughout Social Fabric

II. How Does Environmental Education Contribute to Environmental Problem Solving and Management?

A. Tbilisi Declaration

    1. Result of the World's First Intergovernmental Conference on Environmental Education

    2. Goals for Environmental Education

        a. Encourage Students to Consider Environment as Whole

        b. Integrate Knowledge from the Disciplines

        c. Consider Short- and Long-Term Effects of Solutions to Problems

B. EE Recognized as System Developed for the Purpose of Awakening and Exploring Personal Values

C. Can Encourage View of Nature as Living Entity that Can Benefit from Concern and Attention

Learning Objectives

After learning the material in Chapter 28 you should be able to:

1. Define environmental education as it first appeared in *Environmental Education*.

2. Outline the overall objectives and purpose of environmental education programs.

3. Describe the goals of environmental education, as outlined during the 1977 World Intergovernmental Conference on Environmental Education.

4. List the educational goals of an environmental curriculum based upon the cognitive thought processes.

5. Contrast the two distinctive approaches to teaching environmental education used by schools today, and list their associated advantages/disadvantages.

6. Identify the Tbilisi Declaration and its importance to environmental education.

> A survey by the National Wildlife Federation found that 90 percent of students believe they and their classmates do not know enough about environmental problems and solutions.

Key Concepts

Read this summary of Chapter 28 and identify the important concepts discussed in the chapter.

Environmental education seeks to awaken and explore a person's values. It is aimed at producing a citizenry knowledgeable about the environment and its associated problems, aware of how to help solve those problems, and motivated to work toward their solution. Educators generally agree that environmental education should be a multidisciplinary program incorporated into the curriculum in all grades.

In order to develop an environmentally aware and concerned citizenry, educators must convey an appreciation for the natural world, an understanding of the structure and function of nature, and a mastery of problem-solving skills. Some teachers advocate adding a separate environmental field to the curriculum. Others advocate making environmental issues an integral part of all courses in the curriculum.

Many groups outside of the formal school system are important targets for environmental education because their actions or inaction can influence local environmental quality. Informal programs encompass a broad array of educational approaches at diverse sites. As with formal educational programs, informal programs are increasingly developed around problem-oriented objectives.

The Tbilisi Declaration resulted from the world's first intergovernmental conference on environmental education. The declaration's goals illustrate how education can and does contribute to environmental problem solving and management.

Environmental Success Story

After reading brochures about the environmental effects of plastic, a group of students from Ocean City, Maryland decided to clean up a nearby beach. The fourth, fifth, and sixth graders first came up with an informative flyer that included statistics and facts about the effects of plastic and other trash on the environment. They presented a slide show to other students and did public service announcements on their local TV network in order to inform the community of the planned cleanup. A variety of people throughout the community showed up on the cleanup day ready to work. In only an hour and a half, the group picked up around 100 large bags full of garbage. As a result of their great success in cleaning up Assateague Island, they now have a STOP (Students Tackle Ocean Plastic) cleanup every year. After three successful cleanups, some of the STOP members were asked to do a year-long "debris survey" for the Center for Marine Conservation.

True/False

1. All states require environmental education to be taught in secondary schools.   T   F

2. The EPA Office of Environmental Education flourished and expanded during the Reagan administration.   T   F

3. One disadvantage of having separate environmental education courses is that students may not be able to see how the topics relate to the rest of their lives.   T   F

4. Many national and international conservation organizations offer informal education programs.   T   F

5. Environmental education, if properly taught, can be limited to school children and those in college; it is not needed by the general populace.   T   F

Fill in the Blank

1. _____ seeks to awaken and explore a person's values; it is aimed at producing a citizenry knowledgeable about the environment and its associated problems, aware of how to help solve those problems, and motivated to work toward their solution.

2. _____ sponsors scientists, teachers, and artists undertaking research designed to improve human understanding of the planet, the diversity of its inhabitants, and the quality of life on earth.

3. Members of Kids for Saving Earth (KSE) work to educate their families and friends about the three R's: _____, _____, and _____.

4. _____ is a program focused on organic gardening offered by the New Alchemy Institute of Massachusetts for use in elementary schools.

5. Three states mandate environmental education in schools; they are _____, _____, and _____.

Multiple Choice

Choose the best answer.

1. In what decade did the concept of values become part of the definition of environmental education?
   A. 1960s
   B. 1970s
   C. 1980s
   D. 1990s

2. Which of the following are characteristic of an environmentally aware and concerned citizenry?
   A. appreciation for the natural world
   B. understanding of the structure and function of nature
   C. mastery of problem-solving skills
   D. all of the above

3. Which of the following is a program for college and university level students?
   A. School for Field Studies
   B. Green Classroom
   C. Sunship Earth
   D. Earthkeepers

4. The environmental science programs at Oak Park-River Forest grew out of which of the following?
   A. a state mandate to integrate environmental education into the secondary science curricula
   B. political opposition to the Reagan administration's environmental policies
   C. the enthusiasm of one very special teacher
   D. a conservation workshop held on Earth Day, 1970

5. The EPA Office of Environmental Education is responsible for which of the following?
   A. awarding education grants
   B. creating federal internships
   C. recognizing outstanding environmental achievement through an awards program
   D. all of the above

Short Answer

1. Briefly describe two approaches to adding environmental education to the school curriculum.

2. Name the four broad goals for curriculum development in environmental education.

3. Describe the target groups for informal environmental education and briefly explain why it is important that these groups become environmentally aware.

4. What is "COOL IT!"?

5. Name at least five forums for informal environmental education.

Thought Questions

Develop a complete answer for each of the following.

1. Describe the goals of environmental education, and give examples of ways environmental educators are trying to achieve these goals.

2. Who is contributing to informal environmental education efforts? Describe the kinds of things these groups are doing to make people more environmentally aware.

3. Why are values an important part of environmental education?

4. Discuss how environmental education could be integrated into the following courses: Literature, History, Art, Math, Geography, Social Studies, Physics, and Chemistry.

5. Differentiate between formal and informal environmental education. What are the advantages and disadvantages of each? Which do you think is most effective and why?

Related Concepts

Describe the relationship.   (There may be more than one.)

BETWEEN...	AND...
formal environmental education	informal environmental education
Tbilisi Declaration	environmentally sound management
global ethic	environmental education
discrete environmental course	environmental education integrated into other courses
environmental education	a sense of wonder

Did You Know ... ?

Schools buy more books than anyone else in the United States, but practically no textbooks are printed on recycled paper. (*Biosphere 2000: Protecting Our Global Environment* is printed on recycled paper!)

Suggested Activities

1. Urge the PTA of a local school to set up an environment committee and endorse an environmental curriculum.

2. Conduct a campus-wide environmental audit to identify opportunities to minimize waste generation, reduce water and air pollution, and conserve energy and water.

3. Urge your student government to pass resolutions supporting environmentalism.

4. Create a coalition of campus groups to promote environmental issues.

5. Organize an environmental teach-in on Earth Day (April 22).

Special Supplement

Guidelines for Research

This section of the learning guide was written to help students who have been given the assignment of a research paper, term paper, or other research project in environmental problem solving and environmentally sound management. Although most students probably had some experience with this in high school, many students get to college without ever having performed a research project and are intimidated by the prospect of one. If you are in this situation now, you may have a lot of questions: *How do I choose a subject? How do I use the library? Where do I look for information? How much information is enough? What should I discuss in my research paper?*

Don't panic. This section gives answers to these and other questions in the form of guidelines. If you follow these guidelines, you will be able to conduct research successfully.

This guide gives you a thorough, step-by-step process for researching, but it is not exhaustive. You will undoubtedly discover other sources of information specific to your topic. Don't hesitate to use them. For example, as you read an article on radioactive waste disposal in *New Scientist*, you find the name of a prominent scientist who is an expert on the subject. Find out where she can be reached, and contact her to request an interview.

As the preceding example suggests, the research process does not necessarily begin and end in the library. Some of your most valuable sources of information will be your own experiences and the experiences of other people—especially experts on your subject.

Most of the reference materials mentioned in this guide are fairly common and easy to find at college and university libraries. In addition, almost every library has many resources not mentioned here. Work closely with your library staff to locate useful materials.

Choose a Subject

The first task in your research strategy is choosing a subject to research. The subject you choose will determine how and where you will look for the information, and how much information you will find. Your subject should be

- Of Interest to You. Would you like to learn about the economic effects of a fossil fuel shortage? Are you interested in public education on the loss of

288

tropical rain forests? Do you want to investigate the health effects of toxic waste? Your enthusiasm will take you a long way toward a successful project.

- Worthy of Research.   If you choose a subject that is trivial, you won't be able to find enough information on it.

- Specific. Too broad a topic will result in information overload and badly organized research. For example, acid precipitation is a global problem, so "acid rain" is probably too broad a subject. Some initial investigation into the topic, though, will reveal that acid rain is a particular problem in the Adirondacks of the U.S. Acid rain in the Adirondacks is a better subject.

- Not Too Specific.   If your subject is obscure or narrow your library may not have any information on it. For example, the effects of a particular chemical on a particular species is probably too specific, but the effects of toxic chemicals on a particular ecosystem is probably not.

How do you know if you've chosen a good subject? Your instructor and your librarian are good people to discuss it with. They will have a good idea of the information that is available and whether or not your subject is too broad or too narrow.

After you have chosen a subject, head for the library and read general discussions on the resource. A good place to start is with the science dictionaries and textbooks. Science encyclopedias, such as the *McGraw-Hill Encyclopedia of Environmental Science* and the *McGraw-Hill Encyclopedia of Science and Technology*, can be found in the reference section. Read the information on that topic in your textbook. Reference materials (encyclopedias) and general materials (textbooks) will give you a good overview of the issues related to your subject, and will help you narrow it down to a more workable size, if necessary.

Don't overlook two very important sources of help at this stage: your instructor and your librarian. Both are well qualified to help you in your search.

Use these and other books (including textbooks) to gain a basic understanding of your subject.

- *Grzimek's Encyclopedia of Ecology.* Bernhard Grzimek, Joachim Illies, Wolfgang Klausewitz, editors.

   A collection of essays that provides a good introduction to various environmental topics.

- *McGraw-Hill Encyclopedia of Environmental Science*, 2nd edition. Sybil P. Parker, editor. 1980. New York: McGraw-Hill Book Co.

  A good collection of introductory essays.

Develop an Outline

After you've chosen a subject, develop an outline. We suggest using the same approach as Biosphere 2000:

I. <u>Describing the Resource</u>.
   Begin with a comprehensive description of the resource. Describe all physical, biological and social boundaries, such as resource availability, wildlife, and cultural beliefs and values .

II. <u>History of Management of the Resource</u>.
   Provide a historical account of previous management practices. Include an analysis of successful and unsuccessful practices. Your research for this section will call for investigation into the technologies and government policies associated with the resource.

III. <u>Future Management of the Resource</u>.
   Develop a plan for future management. This is the heart of environmentally sound management. Your personal discovery is worthwhile, because as you develop a management plan, you will begin to understand what needs to be done, on a personal as well as societal level, to manage resources wisely.

The outline doesn't have to be detailed at this point, just enough to help you organize your research. You probably will add a second level of detail after reading a couple of encyclopedia articles or textbooks. You'll add additional levels of detail as you get more information.

Begin Your Research

Once you have chosen a subject, narrowed it down to a manageable size, and developed an outline, you are ready to begin your research. The following information describes how to locate the primary types of research materials found in libraries: books and periodicals.

Library of Congress Subject Headings

The Library of Congress publishes a list of all the **subject headings** used in libraries. This list is the key to using the card catalog and many other indexing tools because it tells you the correct subject headings to use. Ask your librarian to help you use it.

The list will save you a lot of time and frustration if you use it before you use the card catalog.

Below are examples of the subject headings you might find.

Subject You've Chosen	Subject Headings in the Card Catalog
Endangered species	EXTINCT ANIMALS RARE ANIMALS RARE BIRDS WILDLIFE CONSERVATION PLANT CONSERVATION RARE PLANTS
Pesticides and pest management	PESTICIDES HERBICIDES INSECTICIDES PESTICIDES AND WILDLIFE AGRICULTURAL CHEMICALS
Offshore drilling	OFFSHORE OIL INDUSTRY COASTAL ZONE MANAGEMENT DRILLING PLATFORMS MARINE POLLUTION COASTAL ECOLOGY

Card Catalog

The card catalog is a valuable tool for locating books and reports. It is the index to the books that the library owns, and it provides information on where these books can be found on the shelves. You can locate this information by using the three types of cards in the catalog — author, title and subject heading cards. In your early research you will probably not know any specific titles or authors and will need to look up books by the subject heading. The subject headings are the phrases you looked up in the *Library of Congress Subject Headings*.

Periodical Indexes

Books provide useful information, but they take a while to write and publish. If you want to find the most recent information (and you do) then you need to look for journal articles. Many journals are published weekly or monthly, so their information is very up-to-date. A **periodical index** tells you what articles have been published and what journals have published them. Each index is arranged a little differently, but all of them give you the information you need to locate the article you want: author, article title, journal title, volume number, page numbers and date of publication. This information is called the **citation**.

Abstracted indexes can save you a lot of time and effort. They provide the same essential information as the other indexes, but they also provide summaries (abstracts) of the articles indexed. Read these summaries and decide whether or not reading the entire article would aid your research. The index section provides the citation information you'll need to locate the original article.

Periodical indexes frequently have different index sections, such as subject and author indexes. You will probably use subject indexes most often. Which section you use depends on your research needs. For example, if you are looking for information from only one region, see if the index has a geographic index. The same is true if you are searching for a specific author—look for an author index. When you have located a journal article that you want to read, check your library's **serials holdings list**—the list of all the periodicals that the library subscribes to—and find out if that journal is available. Ask your librarian for the holdings list.

Several of the more useful indexes are listed below.

- *Applied Science and Technology Index*
  Bronx: The H.W. Wilson Co.

  This index covers a variety of science and mathematics periodicals. It is most useful for research on energy resources.

- *Biological and Agricultural Index*

- *Environment Index and Environment Abstracts*
  Marc J. Sherman, editor. New York: EIC/Intelligence.

  These two books have indexes and abstracts (summaries) of key environmental literature each month. You can use them to look up subjects, authors and geographic areas. Use the <u>Index</u> to locate the citations that deal with your subject. Then look in the <u>Abstracts</u> for summaries of those sources. If you would like to locate the original article, the books provide the information you need. The <u>Index</u> also has a Review Section which contains essays on major environmental events and problems, a directory of contacts in federal and state agencies, regional commissions and nongovernmental associations, and a list of recent environmental books and films.

- *General Science Index*
  Bronx: The H.W. Wilson Co.

  As the title implies, this is a general index which covers a wide range of topics, including atmospheric science, biology, environment and conservation, food and nutrition, oceanography, and zoology.

- *Pollution Abstracts*

More Periodical Indexes

Some periodical indexes aren't solely for environmental information, but they may still be helpful. A few of these indexes are listed below. The periodical index you choose will depend on the aspect of management you are investigating. For example, if you want to know more about the attitudes of the current administration in Washington, D.C. toward the environment or the economic feasibility of alternative energy sources, you might look in the *Business Periodicals Index*.

Other indexes you can consult are:

- *Education Index*
- *Public Affairs Information Service (PAIS)*
- *Business Periodicals Index*

Bibliographies

Many books and articles have **bibliographies** which will give you additional places to look for information. Always check for a bibliography in any source you use. Then follow up on any books or articles you think might be helpful in your research.

Government Documents

The United States Government is the world's largest publisher. The federal government sponsors a lot of research and publishes the results. These public documents are an invaluable source of information. Government agencies relevant to the environment include the Environmental Protection Agency, the United States Geological Survey, the Department of Energy, the Department of Agriculture, and the Department of the Interior. Publications are listed in the *Monthly Catalog of U.S. Government Publications*, the main index to all U.S. executive, judicial and congressional publications.

All libraries, even the smallest public library, have access to government documents. Some libraries receive government documents regularly—these are the **depositories**. Check with your librarian to find out where the nearest U.S. government document depository is. The regional depository is responsible for making the documents available to other libraries. Your library will contact the depository on your behalf.

NOTE: Government documents are arranged under the Superintendent of Documents (SuDoc) classification system. Reports are classified by the agency which issued them. All Department of Agriculture publications are under the letter A; publications of the Environmental Protection Agency are together under EP. Ask the librarian for assistance.

Other guides to government publications are listed below:

- *American Statistics Index and Abstracts* (ASI). Washington, D.C.: Congressional Information Service, Inc.

  If you need statistical information for the United States, ASI can help you find it. You can use these books to locate information from the many statistical sources published within the federal government. (International statistics are published in several publications of the United Nations.)

- *Monthly Catalog of U.S. Government Publications*. Washington, D.C.: U.S. Government Printing Office.

  This index covers almost all government publications, including House and Senate hearings, bills and laws, and research reports. The Environmental Protection Agency publishes many reports on environmental research; the Department of Energy and the Department of Agriculture also publish relevant materials. Other useful materials are published by the National Park Service and U. S. Forestry Service.

- Congressional Information Service (CIS Index). Washington, D.C.: Congressional Information Service, Inc.

  The CIS Index provides information (including abstracts) on congressional reports. You can use these to find information on environmental legislation.

- *National Technical Information Service (NTIS Reports indexes).*

  NTIS reports are government funded research reports. These reports come from universities, corporations and research foundations and cover many subject areas. Use the <u>Government Reports Announcements and Index</u> and the <u>Government Reports Annual Index</u> to identify relevant and useful reports. If your library does not own the report, you may be able to order it. Ask the documents librarian for information.

- *The U.S. Government Manual*

- United Nations Publications

  The United Nations publishes many documents which provide information on foreign countries. The UNDOC indexes all official and non-official publications. Some useful indexes are:

  - *Directory of International Statistics*

  - *World Population Trends*

  - *World Population Prospects*

  - *Handbook of Industrial Statistics*

  - *Energy Statistics Yearbook*

<u>Other sources</u>

- *Dictionary of the Environment*, 2nd edition. Michael Allaby. 1983. New York University Press.

  This helpful dictionary defines terms which concern the environmental sciences.

- *Environmental Glossary*, 3rd edition. G. William Frick, editor. 1984. Rockville, MD: Government Institutes, Inc.

  This glossary defines the terms which are used in federal statutes and also provides an explanation of basic regulatory concepts used by the Environmental Protection Agency.

Don't overlook newspapers as a source for recent and regional information. Ask the librarian to help you with the newspaper files. Find articles on local issues and events which concern your subject. Was there a chemical spill in your area? Find the news reports on it. Did your hometown recently institute a pollution clean-up plan? Look for the local press coverage.

For issues on a national or international level, the *New York Times Index* is a good place to start.

Take Notes

As you read about your subject, take notes. Organize your notes according to your outline. A good way to manage this is to keep a notebook with tabs for each of your major headings, and put your notes behind the appropriate tab.

Helpful Hint: Don't write the author's exact words in your notebook in your own handwriting. If you do, when the time comes to write about it, you may not remember whether you paraphrased or not. If you think you may want to quote a source, photocopy that page and put it into your notebook. Otherwise, always paraphrase the information you jot down in your notes. It will make it a lot easier when you start writing, and you won't inadvertently plagiarize.

Cite Your Sources

As you take notes, be sure to keep careful track of the reference materials you use. You will need to give credit to all of the sources you use in your research, according to the citation rules that your instructor prefers. If you wait until you are ready to type your paper to begin recording citations, chances are you will forget some of your sources. You will have to make several return trips to the library to look up missing information.

To avoid having to do your research over again, keep information on all your sources in your notebook. For books, record the author, title, date of publication, publisher, city, and page numbers. For journal articles, record the author, article title, journal title, volume number, issue number, page numbers, and date. You don't have to worry about the format of this information now, but you'll be glad that you have it when the time comes to type it later.

If you plan to use direct quotes, be sure to record them accurately. A good way to ensure that you've gotten the quote right is to photocopy the section from the original text. The more you recopy text by hand (or by typewriter or word processor) the more likely you are to incorporate errors into the quotation.

IMPORTANT: You must give citations for any information that you use in your paper. You are probably aware that if you use direct quotes, you must provide references to the sources. You must also provide citations for paraphrased material. If you don't give proper credit, you will be guilty of plagiarism.

Sources Outside the Library

There is a wealth of information which cannot be found on a bookshelf. By venturing outside the library, you can not only get information relating to your subject, but you will also get an interesting view of various types of organizations-- public and private. Many groups will supply you with materials for free or for a nominal fee.

Four sources are especially important:

- Individuals with special interests in environmental science and environmentally sound management

- Environmental organizations

- Governmental organizations

- Private environmental research and management firms

Contacting Individuals with Special Interests

There are two ways that individuals with special interests may aid you in your research. They may act as sources for information (either through an interview or by providing you with written information) or they may act as reviewers, checking the information that you have compiled.

Many environmental scientists and resource managers who are concerned about the environment are very willing to help students learn about their areas of expertise. But remember that their time is valuable. In other words, be prepared and as well informed as possible before you approach them. A letter or a brief phone call can introduce you with a request for information or an interview. Tell them that you are a student who is interested in environmental management and explain why you would like information.

If the person is willing to be interviewed, arrange a time for an interview, either over the phone or in person. Prepare a list of questions to guide the interview (but don't limit yourself to these). Take notes during the interview and, if possible, tape the session to transcribe later.

If an interview is not possible, then request written information. The person may be willing to send you information that is not available at your library.

Contacting Environmental and Governmental Organizations

Environmental and governmental organizations are invaluable sources of information. Write or call for printed materials on your subject. The Sierra Club, The Nature Conservancy, World Wildlife Fund and The Conservation Foundation are just some of the environmental organizations which may provide you with useful information. The Environmental Protection Agency, the Department of Agriculture and the Department of Energy are only a few of the many helpful government organizations. The United Nations can also supply information.

At the state level, you can contact the state Environmental Protection Agency and natural resources and health departments.

Contacting Private Research and Resource Management Firms

Many private firms conduct research related to the environment and can provide you with information on their work. Locate firms which are involved with your resource and contact them. If, for example, you are researching the handling of radioactive materials, you might contact a company such as Westinghouse, which performs research in this area. Request information which could help you form your management plan. (Be aware, however, that some information is proprietary, and firms will not release it.)

Write Your Paper

With your research done, you're ready to write. Follow the outline you used for your research. Find out from your instructor if he or she has a preference for a particular style for such things as footnotes and bibliographic citations. If not, we suggest you purchase an inexpensive style guide for research papers. Several should be available at your campus bookstore. Most of these books also provide writing tips. When writing your first draft, include all the information that comes to mind. If your paper is too long, you can go back later and edit. Revise your work until you are satisfied.

The hard part is over. At this point, you just need to make sure that the paper you hand in looks like you worked on it as hard as you did. If you use word processing software to type your paper, use a spell checker to correct typographical errors and misspellings. To make doubly sure you catch errors, proofread a printed copy. Better yet, have a friend proofread it.

Finally, turn it in . . . on time.

ANSWER SECTION

Chapter 1

True/False
1. F
2. F
3. F
4. T
5. T

Fill in the Blank
1. 80
2. pollutant
3. anthropocentric
4. stewards (responsible for caring for the earth)
5. industrialization and urbanization

Multiple Choice
1. B
2. D
3. D
4. C
5. A

Short Answer
1. Spaceship Earth is an analogy used by environmentalists in the 60s and 70s that described earth as a closed system with finite resources and limited ability to recycle pollution.
2. Biocentric worldview sees humans and human culture as part of nature; anthropocentric worldview sees humans and human culture (buildings, social institutions, etc.) as separate from nature.
3. Living organisms live at the expense of their environment, have cellular structure, reproduce, respond to stimuli, show growth, and evolve and adapt. Most also exhibit movement.
4. Renewable resources are those that can be replaced by the environment if they are not used up faster than they can be restored. Nonrenewable resources are those that are in finite supply or are replaced so slowly that they may as well be finite.
5. Net primary productivity is the total amount of solar energy fixed biologically through photosynthesis minus the amount of energy that plants use for their own needs.

Chapter 2

True/False
1. F
2. F
3. T
4. F
5. F

Fill in the Blank
1. population size, available resource base, culture
2. scientific method
3. ecosystem
4. Litigation
5. stewardship ethic

Multiple Choice
1. C
2. C
3. B
4. C
5. D

Short Answer
1. A sustainable earth society is in harmony with natural systems and maintains the health and integrity of the environment. A sustaining earth society nurtures and supports the diversity of life.
2. Controlled experiments and reporting of methods and results to other scientists (who may repeat the experiment)
3. An ecosystem is a self-sustaining community of organisms interacting with one another and with the physical environment within a given geographic area.
4. Ecology is important for understanding the structure and function of ecosystems. Theology, education, and art each are important for the shaping of worldviews. Theology helps us understand human motivations and how we answer questions about our origins. Education shapes opinions and perceptions and is a means of sharing information. Art can encourage or discourage stewardship by expressing the value placed on the natural world and the relationship between natural and cultural systems.
5. 1) Identify and diagnose the problem.
   2) Set goals and objectives.
   3) Design and conduct a study.
   4) Propose alternative solutions.
   5) Implement, monitor, and re-evaluate the chosen solution.

Chapter 3

True/False
1. F
2. F
3. F
4. T
5. T

Fill in the Blank
1. habitat
2. abiota and biota
3. compounds
4. macronutrients
5. primary consumers or herbivores
6. detritivores or detritus feeders

Multiple Choice
1. B
2. D
3. D
4. A
5. B

Short Answer
1. individual, species, population, community, ecosystem, biome, biosphere
2. the tendency of energy to disperse and become less ordered
3. different forms of the same atom with varying numbers of neutrons
4. carbon, oxygen, hydrogen, nitrogen, phosphorus, sulfur
5. when human activities lead to nutrient enrichment of a body of water

Chapter 4

True/False
1. T
2. F
3. T
4. F
5. F

Fill in the Blank

1. phytoplankton
2. respiration
3. Nitrogen fixation
4. carbon, oxygen, nitrogen
5. global warming

Multiple Choice

1. A
2. D
3. C
4. C

Short Answer

1. the release of energy from fuel molecules
2. a model that depicts the production, use, and transfer of energy from one trophic level to another.
3. a model that depicts the relative abundance of organisms at each trophic level; carnivores at the top are relatively few in number
4. a model that depicts the relative amounts of biomass at each trophic level. There is less biomass at higher trophic levels. (The organisms are larger in size, but there are fewer of them.)
5. Trees and other plants use carbon dioxide in the process of photosynthesis. Oceans dissolve it, and it may there combine with calcium or magnesium to eventually form limestone or dolomite.

Chapter 5

True/False

1. T
2. T
3. F
4. F
5. T

Fill in the Blank

1. ecosystem succession or ecosystem development
2. inertia
3. endoparasite
4. lag phase
5. carrying capacity

Multiple Choice
1. A
2. C
3. D
4. D
5. B

Short Answer
1. any change in the environment of an ecosystem. It is a disturbance that alters the ecosystems; examples are climatic changes, natural disasters, human activities.
2. association of organisms best adapted to the physical conditions of a geographic area; usually dominated by a few abundant plant species, e.g., beech-maple forest
3. Primary succession occurs where no organisms previously existed (e.g., bare rock). Secondary succession occurs where the ecosystem has been disturbed.
4. Pioneer organisms begin the process of soil formation in primary succession. Their organic detritus mixes with bits of weathered rock. The primitive soil they create enables other organisms to move in.
5. the principle that operates when interspecific competition leads to the exclusion of one of the competing species

Chapter 6

True/False
1. T
2. T
3. F
4. F
5. T

Fill in the Blank
1. damage, disruption, destruction, desertification, deforestation
2. disruption
3. Destruction
4. point
5. cross-media pollutant

Multiple Choice
1. B
2. D
3. A
4. B
5. D

Short Answer
1. quantity, persistence, effect, time to remove, how the pollutant enters the environment
2. when substances interact to create an effect greater than the sum of their individual effects (e.g., photochemical smog, chloromines, interaction of chemicals in landfills)
3. grasslands and agricultural lands (especially semi-arid and arid)
4. conversion to agricultural use or pasture land; demand for fuel, timber, and paper products; construction of roadways
5. the delay between the time a chronic pollutant is introduced to the environment and the time its effects are noticed

Chapter 7

True/False
1. F
2. T
3. T
4. F
5. T

Fill in the Blank
1. disturbance ecology
2. Landscape ecology
3. indicator species
4. agroecology
5. conservation, preservation

Multiple Choice
1. B
2. C
3. B
4. B
5. A

Short Answer
1. disturbance ecology, landscape ecology, agroecology, ecotoxicology, conservation ecology, and restoration ecology
2. Applied ecology involves using scientific knowledge to <u>manage</u> natural systems. It therefore must incorporate societal values. Ecology, on the other hand, strictly enhances knowledge about structure and function of communities.

3. (1) to maintain present diversity of species and ecosystems, (2) to repair biotic communities after a disturbance, (3) to increase knowledge of biotic communities and restoration techniques
4. application of ecological principles to conserve species and communities
5. Agroecosystems are less complex and diverse; they also require inputs of water, energy, and nutrients.

Chapter 8

True/False
1. T
2. F
3. T
4. F
5. F

Fill in the Blank
1. crude birth rate
2. replacement fertility
3. Population momentum
4. gross national product (GNP)
5. infant mortality rate

Multiple Choice
1. B
2. C
3. C
4. A
5. D

Short Answer
1. actual population increase = (births + immigration) − (deaths + emigration)
2. zero population growth is when the number of deaths equals the number of births, and immigration equals emigration; that is, no growth occurs in absolute numbers
3. the number of years it will take for a population to double in size; calculated by the
   rule of 70: 70 ∏ current growth rate = number of years to double (assuming growth rate remains constant)

4. The general fertility rate is the number of live births per 1000 women of childbearing age (15-49) per year. The age-specific fertility rate is the same as above, but for a specific age group. The total fertility rate is the average number of children a woman will bear during her life (based on age-specific rate).
5. population density, urbanization, life expectancy, infant mortality rate, childhood mortality rate

Chapter 9

True/False
1. F
2. T
3. F
4. F
5. T

Fill in the Blank
1. demographic transition
2. population policy
3. Family planning
4. preconception
5. demographic trap

Multiple Choice
1. C
2. C
3. C
4. A
5. A

Short Answer
1. the U.S. government's policy of prohibiting funding for organizations involved in abortion-related activities or for countries where family planning activities are deemed coercive
2. a wide variety of measures, including education in hygiene, human sexuality, prenatal and postnatal care, and birth control; the goal is to enable couples to have the number of healthy children they want
3. teenagers and poor women
4. rise in living standards due to the Industrial Revolution, safe and inexpensive means of birth control, and an increase in the cost of child rearing

5. Stage 1: birth and death rates are both high
   Stage 2: death rates fall but birth rates remain high
   Stage 3: birth rates begin to fall and growth rate approaches zero
   Stage 4: population growth rate continues to decline to zero or a negative rate

Chapter 10

True/False
1. F
2. T
3. F
4. T
5. F

Fill in the Blank
1. Carbohydrates and fats
2. fisheries
3. Malabsorptive hunger
4. land races
5. cryopreservation

Multiple Choice
1. B
2. B
3. B
4. A
5. C

Short Answer
1. Proteins form muscles, organs, antibodies, and enzymes. They are needed for growth, especially fetal development.
2. wheat, rice, maize (corn), potato
3. widespread starvation
4. a region of various nations in southeast Asia, the Indian subcontinent, the Middle East, Africa, and Latin America where most of the world's hungry live
5. infant mortality rate, life expectancy at age 1, literacy rate

Chapter 11

True/False
1. F
2. T
3. T
4. F
5. F

Fill in the Blank
1. conventional resources
2. Renewable
3. Energy efficiency
4. life-cycle cost
5. "Drain America First"

Multiple Choice
1. D
2. B
3. B
4. D
5. C

Short Answer
1. Their net efficiency is only about 5%; that is, about 95% of the electrical energy is converted to heat.
2. initial cost + lifetime operating cost
3. the percentage of total energy input that does useful work and is not converted into low quality heat
4. a nation's overall approach to energy resources, including both the kind and amount of energy used
5. Also known as the law of conservation of energy, it states that energy can be neither created nor destroyed, but it can be changed or converted in form.

Chapter 12

True/False
1. F
2. F
3. F
4. T
5. T

Fill in the Blank

1. 300; Carboniferous
2. sunlight; photosynthesis
3. proven (economic) resources
4. anthracite
5. cogeneration

Multiple Choice
1. C
2. B
3. C
4. D
5. A

Short Answer
1. Dead plants sank to the bottom of wetlands and were compressed by increasing layers of water and sediments.
2. Aquatic organisms (algae and plankton) sank to the bottom of shallow, nutrient-rich seas. Heat from the earth's interior and the pressure from overlying sediments produced the conditions for the formation of oil.
3. Increasing amounts of heat, pressure, and anaerobic decomposition turned organic matter into natural gas.
4. about 3,000; gasoline
5. coal that has been heated in an airtight oven; it is burned with iron ore and limestone to produce pure iron for steel

Chapter 13

True/False
1. F
2. F
3. T
4. T
5. T

Fill in the Blank
1. uranium-235
2. convection, conduction, radiation
3. 13 m.p.h.
4. dry steam, wet steam, hot water
5. bagasse

Multiple Choice

1. B
2. B
3. D
4. B
5. A

Short Answer

1. The atom undergoes fission; it splits, produces smaller atoms, more free neutrons, and heat.
2. Deuterium oxide, or heavy water, is used as a coolant in heavy water reactors because it does not absorb neutrons readily.
3. a central receiving system, usually a tall tower, in which gas or fluid is heated by the sun to power a turbine
4. the use of solid waste to produce energy, often by incineration or methane recovery
5. a tax based on emissions of carbon dioxide; used to encourage the switch from coal to gas or alternative sources to generate electricity

Chapter 14

True/False

1. F
2. F
3. T
4. F
5. T

Fill in the Blank

1. greenhouse gases
2. acid surges
3. photochemical smog
4. rain shadow effect
5. in descending order: thermosphere, mesosphere, stratosphere, troposphere

Multiple Choice

1. D
2. B
3. C
4. A
5. B

Short Answer
1. 78% nitrogen, 21% oxygen, 1% CO_2 and rare gases (helium, argon, krypton)
2. carbon dioxide (CO_2), carbon monoxide (CO), sulfur oxides (SO_x), nitrous oxides (NO_x), hydrocarbons and particulates
3. formaldehyde, radon 222, tobacco smoke, asbestos, combustion products from stoves and furnaces (CO, NO_x, SO_2 and particulates), pesticides and household chemicals, disease-causing organisms or spores
4. radiational cooling, downslope air movements, and high pressure cells
5. wood burning stoves

Chapter 15

True/False
1. T
2. F
3. T
4. T
5. T

Fill in the Blank
1. oligotrophic
2. epilimnion, thermocline, hypolimnion
3. littoral, euphotic, neritic, pelagic, abyssal
4. biological oxygen demand
5. Secondary

Multiple Choice
1. D
2. C
3. C
4. A
5. A

Short Answer
1. the entire runoff area of a particular body of water
2. warm water, sandy or muddy bottom, low dissolved oxygen content, high productivity
3. confirmed—the material above it is permeable; confined—an impermeable layer prevents or restricts water flow
4. the water that leaves a wastewater treatment facility
5. chlorine—to kill bacteria; quicklime—to reduce acidity and prevent corrosion; fluoride—to prevent tooth decay

Chapter 16

True/False
1. F
2. T
3. F
4. T
5. F

Fill in the Blank
1. fertility
2. soil structure, or tilth
3. From top to bottom: A horizon (topsoil), E horizon, B horizon, C horizon, R horizon (bedrock)
4. parent material
5. soil loss tolerance level (also called T-value or replacement level)

Multiple Choice
1. B
2. B
3. D
4. B
5. A

Short Answer
1. on average 45% minerals, 25% waters, 25% air, and 5% humus
2. loams—40% silt, 40% sand, 20% clay; good aeration and water retention/drainage
   clays—can become waterlogged and deficient in oxygen
   sands—too porous to retain sufficient moisture for plant growth
3. parent material, climate, topography, living organisms, time
4. cultivation of marginal or poor cropland and use of poor farming techniques on good cropland
5. growing a mixture of self-sustaining (perennial) crops that do not require new plantings each year

Chapter 17

True/False
1. T
2. F
3. F
4. F
5. F

Fill in the Blank
1. magma
2. ore
3. Overburden
4. strategic
5. stockpiles

Multiple Choice
1. B
2. B
3. A
4. D
5. D

Short Answer
1. igneous rock—cooled and solidified magma
   sedimentary rock—compacted sediments
   metamorphic rock—rocks deep below earth's surface that are heated until the original crystal structure is lost and that recrystallize as they cool
2. fuels-
   nonfuels-
          metallic-characterized by malleability, ductility, thermal conductivity
          nonmetallic-not possessing the above qualities
3. critical minerals—essential to economic activity; strategic minerals—essential to the nation's defense
4. a United Nations treaty (unratified) that establishes exclusive economic zones that are under the control of coastal nations; also establishes an International Seabed Authority to license mining companies and collect taxes on minerals
5. an advanced material that is a matrix of one material reinforced with fibers or dispersions of another

Chapter 18

True/False
1. T
2. T
3. F
4. T
5. F

Fill in the Blank
1. half-life
2. radioactive fallout

3. irradiation
4. thorium
5. decommissioned

Multiple Choice
1. D
2. B
3. A
4. B
5. C

Short Answer
1. a severe drop in global temperature expected after a nuclear war; caused by soot, smoke, and debris blocking the sunlight
2. Pittsburgh, Pennsylvania (the Shippingport Atomic Power Station)
3. U.S. and Soviet Union would not provide nuclear weapons to other countries, nor would they assist other countries in developing them; also agreed to facilitate the development of peaceful uses of nuclear energy
4. when the reactor core of a nuclear power plant becomes so hot that the fuel rods melt, burning through the containment vessel and boring into the earth
5. plutonium-uranium extraction facility, a reprocessing plant (Hanford, WA) where plutonium and uranium were separated from other fission products

Chapter 19

True/False
1. T
2. T
3. T
4. F
5. F

Fill in the Blank
1. teratogenic
2. chemical, petroleum-refining, metals-processing
3. solidification
4. secure landfills
5. Superfund

Multiple Choice
1. B
2. D
3. C
4. C
5. B

Short Answer

1. Toxic substances have the potential to cause injury to living organisms. When the possibility exists that plants or animals will be exposed to them, they are considered hazardous substances.
2. an illness characterized by an intolerance of one or more classes of chemicals; in some cases, sufferers must live in near isolation from synthetic compounds
3. clay or chalk layer between landfill and aquifer, waterproof plastic lining on the sides and bottom (and sometimes the top), leachate collection system, clay cap
4. a system that brings together companies that have waste and companies that want to use it
5. ignitable, corrosive, reactive, TCLP wastes (toxicity characteristic leaching procedure)

Chapter 20

True/False

1. T
2. F
3. T
4. F
5. T

Fill in the Blank

1. newsprint
2. cullet
3. tipping fee
4. refuse-derived fuel incinerator
5. precycling

Multiple Choice

1. A
2. B
3. C
4. B
5. C

Short Answer

1. agriculture and mining
2. PET, HDPE, and polystyrene
3. Cellulolytic bacteria separate the cellulose (a complex sugar) from wood and paper; acidogens ferment the cellulose into weak acids; methanogens convert the acids into carbon dioxide and methane.

4. a plastic that is mixed with a biodegradable substance such as cornstarch; not really biodegradable
5. the practice of promoting products based on claims that they help or are benign to the environment

Chapter 21

True/False
1. F
2. T
3. T
4. F
5. F

Fill in the Blank
1. National Resource Lands
2. nonconsumptive, recreational use
3. 1906 Antiquities
4. President's Commission on Americans Outdoors
5. National Parks

Multiple Choice
1. D
2. C
3. B
4. B
5. B

Short Answer
1. agency responsible for managing six million acres for water development projects (mostly irrigation) in the western U.S.
2. a situation in which the government owns the land, but private citizens or companies own the minerals beneath its surface
3. a stamp that hunters are required to purchase each year; proceeds are used for the acquisition and maintenance of refuges
4. outdoor recreation, range, timber, watershed, wildlife and fish habitat
5. 1916 Organic Act

Chapter 22

True/False
1. F
2. T
3. T
4. F
5. T

Fill in the Blank
1. 1964 Wilderness Preservation Act
2. Wilderness Society
3. wilderness study area
4. de facto wilderness
5. Memorandum of Understanding

Multiple Choice
1. B
2. C
3. A
4. C
5. D

Short Answer
1. requires any individual who exists in it to depend exclusively on personal efforts for survival; it would preserve as nearly as possible the primitive environment (thus barring roads, power transportation, and settlement); large size
2. former president of the Wilderness Society, author of the 1964 Wilderness Act
3. (1) perpetuate long-lasting, high-quality wilderness for future generations; (2) provide opportunities for public use and enjoyment; (3) allow indigenous wildlife to develop through natural processes; (4) maintain watersheds and airsheds in a healthy condition; (5) maintain primitive character of wilderness as a benchmark for ecological studies
4. Roadless Area Review and Evaluation, conducted by the Forest Service in 1972 (and again in 1977—RARE II); in order to recommend areas for wilderness designation
5. Wild lands of sufficient size can preserve ecosystem diversity, species diversity, and genetic diversity. They also protect airsheds and watersheds and are valuable for many research purposes.

Chapter 23

True/False
1. T
2. F
3. F
4. T
5. F

Fill in the Blank
1. genetic diversity
2. Genetic erosion
3. hybrids
4. charismatic megafauna
5. Heirloom plants

Multiple Choice
1. D
2. A
3. C
4. D
5. B

Short Answer
1. The total number of species is unknown. Estimates range from 5 to 100 million; the figure is probably closer to the high end of that range (mostly microbes and insects).
2. tropical rain forests, coral reefs
3. usually endangered mammals or birds that are valued and receive funding and media attention
4. taxonomic grouping—the practice at some zoos of grouping animals of the same genus together (e.g. cats, primates)
   climatic grouping—practice of grouping animals by biomes (e.g., tropical forest, savanna)
   zoogeographic grouping—practice of grouping animals on the basis of the broad geographic area in which they live, with an emphasis on ecology and habitat (e.g., Africa, Australasia)
5. International Species Inventory System, a computer-based information system for wild animal species in captivity; used to prevent inbreeding

Chapter 24

True/False
1. F
2. T
3. T
4. T
5. F

Fill in the Blank
1. Historic preservation
2. nonmaterial or living
3. Acculturation
4. intrinsic
5. National Register of Historic Places

Multiple Choice
1. C
2. A
3. B
4. D
5. C

Short Answer
1. Historic preservation is for the preservation of material culture only (buildings, art, tools, etc.). Cultural resources management preserves both material and nonmaterial culture (folklore, customs, language, etc.).
2. Acid precipitation weakens and corrodes marble and limestone. Combined with ultraviolet light, it weakens cellulose fibers in wood while the UV light decomposes the lignin that holds the cellulose fibers together.
3. Antiquities Act
4. United Nations Educational, Scientific, and Cultural Organization, an international agency whose purpose is to protect the global cultural heritage
5. a list of cultural and natural properties of universal value, determined by UNESCO's World Heritage Committee

Chapter 25

True/False
1. T
2. F
3. T
4. T
5. F

Fill in the Blank
1. land
2. immanence
3. Amish
4. frontier
5. Pacific yew tree

Multiple Choice
1. C
2. B
3. D
4. C
5. A

Short Answer

1. personal interpretation of religious teachings, how strictly people adhere to their beliefs, personal ethic and morals (not necessarily based on religious beliefs)
2. interfaith Christian organization that has proposed an Eleventh Commandment to define humankind's proper relationship with nature
3. (1) celebration of the cycle of life; (2) immanence, or the divine embodied in the living world and its components; (3) interconnection, or the relatedness of all things
4. system or code of morals that governs attitudes and behaviors
5. *E. coli* is used as the receiving organism for genes in recombinant DNA technology. It also is used to carry genes into the DNA of other, more complex organisms, such as plants.

Chapter 26

True/False

1. T
2. F
3. T
4. T
5. F

Fill in the Blank

1. the World Bank
2. Sustainable development
3. nonrenewable
4. research expeditions
5. debt-for-nature swap

Multiple Choice

1. C
2. A
3. C
4. D
5. C

Short Answer

1. Green taxes, also called environmental taxes, are fees added to the price of products or practices that have high environmental costs.
2. Improving the quality of human life while living within the carrying capacity of supporting ecosystems.
3. An agreement that gives the United Nations the authority to make and enforce decisions on global environmental problems, even without unanimous agreement among nations.

4. Sections of Antarctica are claimed by seven nations--Australia, New Zealand, Soiuth Africa, Norway, Argentina, Chile, and the United Kingdom. Many nations argue for the right to claim Antarctica's vast resources; however, research is the only industry permitted on the continent.
5. One which maintains its natural resource base. A sustainable economy persists and continues to develop by adapting to change and through improvements in knowledge, organization, technology, and wisdom, and is critical to the development of a sustainable society.

Chapter 27

True/False
1. F
2. F
3. F
4. T
5. F

Fill in the Blank
1. litigation; dispute resolution
2. Environmental Protection Agency
3. negligence
4. mediator
5. common law

Multiple Choice
1. D
2. C
3. D
4. D
5. A

Short Answer
1. A court order that requires the defendant to stop or restrict a specified act.
2. nuisance, trespass, and negligence
3. nuisance—unwarranted, unreasonable, or unlawful use of a person's own property that produces annoyance, inconvenience, or material injury to another (for example, smoke blowing from a burning field onto another's property).
4. negligence—failure to exercise the care that "a prudent person" usually takes, resulting in an action or inaction that causes personal or property damage (for example, designing a pipe in such a way that it will eventually leak gas into an underground aquifer).

5. CRMP is a dispute resolution strategy that brings together a team of resource managers and users to develop resource management plans.